PLASTIC CANVAS

101 *Easy* Home Accents™

Edited by Laura Scott

HOUSE of
WHITE
BIRCHES
PUBLISHERS
SINCE 1947

101 Easy Home Accents

Copyright © 2000 House of White Birches, Berne, Indiana 46711

Editor: Laura Scott
Design Manager: Vicki Blizzard
Project Coordinator: Laura Polley
Technical Editor: June Sprunger
Copy Editor: Mary Nowak
Publications Coordinator: Tanya Turner
Technical Artists: Mindy Bell, Leslie Brandt, Julie Catey, Allison Rothe, Jessica Rothe

Photography: Tammy Christian, Jeff Chilcote, Jennifer Fourman
Photography Stylist: Arlou Wittwer
Photography Assistant: Linda Quinlan

Production Coordinator: Brenda Gallmeyer
Book Design: Vicki Macy
Cover Design: Erin Augsburger, Jessi Butler
Graphic Artists: Pam Gregory
Production Assistants: Shirley Blalock, Marj Morgan
Traffic Coordinator: Sandra Beres

Publishers: Carl H. Muselman, Arthur K. Muselman
Chief Executive Officer: John Robinson
Marketing Director: Scott Moss
Book Marketing Manager: Craig Scott
Product Development Director: Vivian Rothe
Publishing Services Manager: Brenda R. Wendling

Printed in the United States of America
First Printing: 2000
Library of Congress Number: 99-95550
ISBN: 1-882138-54-6

A Warm Welcome
from the Editor

*H*ave you ever had someone come into your house, admire a decoration you have, then audibly gasp when you tell them it is made from plastic canvas? Whoever would have thought plastic canvas would evolve past the genre of tissue box covers into this wonderful craft that yes, includes tissue box covers, and so much more!

If someone were to ask me why I love plastic canvas so much, I'd have to say there are three reasons. The first is that it is easy to learn. I stitched my first plastic canvas project when I was eight years old. I didn't have to take a class; I didn't even have to ask my mother for much help. It just made sense. I remember I even changed the design a little bit on that first project (it was a tote bag) to make it more "me." Anyone can learn plastic canvas, from kids to great-grandparents. And, the large holes make it easy for little hands and tired eyes alike to master.

The second reason I love plastic canvas is that it is a relatively inexpensive craft. Sure, you can add beautiful metallic threads and beads that will add to the cost, but you don't have to in order to end up with an attractive project.

The last reason is that plastic canvas is versatile. From table sets to door hangers to wreaths to potpourri holders to our favorite, tissue box covers, you're sure to find many projects in this collection that are both pretty and practical for your home and personal sense of style.

While planning this book, we worked with our designers to create home accents that are attractive and practical. In other words, we've filled this book with projects we would actually use and display in our own homes. And, if we would use them, we figure you'll find items you'll use in your home, too. Of course, you need not limit the use of these projects to dressing up your home. They make wonderful gifts for family and friends, too, for just about any occasion.

Warmest regards,

Laura Scott

Contents

Table-Top Treasures

Sweet-Scents Sensations

Keepsake Decor

Terrific Tissue Toppers

*Tissue box covers are many stitchers' all-time
favorite projects. You'll find a delightful assortment of
covers in this collection of a dozen projects!*

Golden Anchors

Accented with a vibrant red and white checkered border, this tissue box cover features a collection of golden anchors stitched with metallic ribbon!

Design by Joan Green

TAKE NOTE

Skill Level: Beginner

Finished Size: Fits boutique-style tissue box

YOU'LL NEED

- □ 1½ sheets 7-count plastic canvas
- □ Spinrite Bernat Berella "4" worsted weight yarn as listed in color key
- □ ⅛-inch-wide Plastic Canvas 7 Metallic Needlepoint Yarn by Rainbow Gallery as listed in color key
- □ ¹⁄₁₆-inch-wide Plastic Canvas 10 Metallic Needlepoint Yarn by Rainbow Gallery as listed in color key
- □ #16 tapestry needle

PROJECT NOTE

When stitching with navy worsted weight yarn, separate into two 2-ply strands, then put them back together for stitching.

INSTRUCTIONS

1 Cut plastic canvas according to graphs (page 7 and 17).

2 Stitch pieces following graphs and Project Note, working uncoded areas with navy Continental Stitches.

3 When background stitching is completed, work Backstitches and French Knots on sides with ¹⁄₁₆-inch-wide gold metallic yarn; work Backstitches and Straight Stitches on top with ⅛-inch-wide gold metallic yarn.

4 Using navy throughout, Overcast inside edges on top and bottom edges of sides. Whipstitch sides together, then Whipstitch sides to top. ■

COLOR KEY	
Worsted Weight Yarn	**Yards**
■ Scarlet #8933	16
□ White #8942	16
■ Navy #8965	45
Uncoded areas are navy #8965 Continental Stitches	
⅛-Inch Metallic Needlepoint Yarn	
■ Gold #PC1	16
⁄ Gold #PC1 Backstitch and Straight Stitch	
¹⁄₁₆-Inch Metallic Needlepoint Yarn	
⁄ Gold #PM51 Backstitch and Straight Stitch	2
○ Gold #PM51 French Knot	

Color numbers given are for Spinrite Bernat Berella "4" worsted weight yarn and Rainbow Gallery ⅛-inch-wide Plastic Canvas 7 Metallic Needlepoint Yarn and ¹⁄₁₆-inch-wide Plastic Canvas 10 Metallic Needlepoint Yarn.

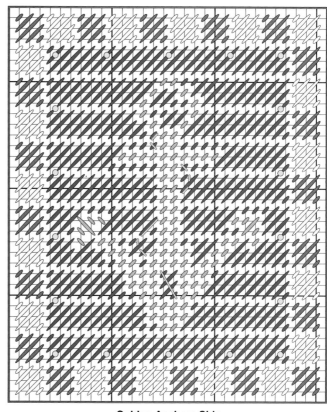

Golden Anchors Side
31 holes x 37 holes
Cut 4

Graphs continued on page 17

English Cottage

Guests in your home will not even realize this decorative cottage is a tissue box cover, too—until they take a close look at the chimney smoke!

Design by Angie Arickx

TAKE NOTE

Skill Level: Beginner

Finished Size: Fits boutique-style tissue box

YOU'LL NEED

- ☐ 2 sheets 7-count plastic canvas
- ☐ Uniek Needloft plastic canvas yarn as listed in color key
- ☐ #16 tapestry needle
- ☐ Hot-glue gun

INSTRUCTIONS

1 Cut plastic canvas according to graphs.

2 Stitch pieces following graphs, working uncoded areas with beige Continental Stitches.

3 Using rose, Overcast top edges of chimney sides, then Whipstitch sides together.

4 Using cerulean throughout, Whipstitch roof sides together; Overcast bottom edges. Whipstitch bottom edges of chimney to top edges of roof.

5 With cinnamon, Overcast top and bottom edges of cottage front and sides, then Whipstitch sides together and to front.

6 Using cerulean, tack roof to sides where indicated on graph. Then secure with a dab of glue. ■

COLOR KEY	
Plastic Canvas Yarn	**Yards**
■ Rose #06	4
■ Cinnamon #14	32
□ Gold #17	5
■ Fern #23	4
■ Cerulean #34	46
■ Watermelon #55	3
■ Pewter #65	8
Uncoded areas are beige #40 Continental Stitches	40
○ Attach roof to side	
Color numbers given are for Uniek Needloft plastic canvas yarn.	

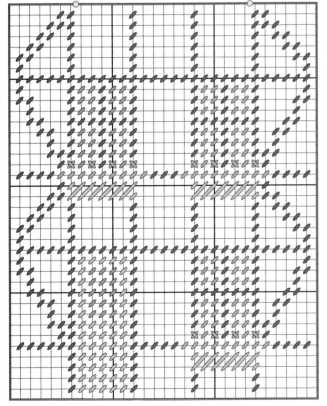

English Cottage Front
30 holes x 37 holes
Cut 1

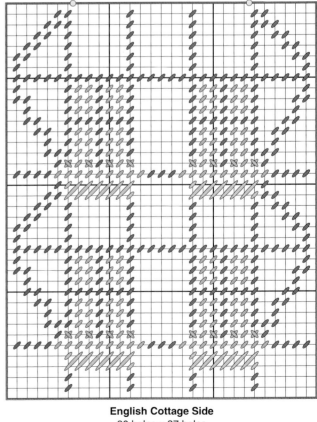

English Cottage Side
30 holes x 37 holes
Cut 3

English Cottage Chimney Side
9 holes x 7 holes
Cut 4

English Cottage Roof Side
39 holes x 25 holes
Cut 4

Springtime Tissue Topper

Celebrate spring's arrival by stitching this tissue topper design
featuring a singing robin, cheery tulips and a white picket fence!

Design by Angie Arickx

TAKE NOTE

Skill Level: Beginner

Finished Size: Fits boutique-style tissue box

YOU'LL NEED

- ☐ 1½ sheets 7-count plastic canvas
- ☐ Uniek Needloft plastic canvas yarn as listed in color key
- ☐ DMC #3 pearl cotton as listed in color key
- ☐ #16 tapestry needle
- ☐ #18 tapestry needle

INSTRUCTIONS

1 Cut plastic canvas according to graphs.

2 With #16 tapestry needle, stitch pieces with yarn following graphs. Work fern Straight Stitches when background stitching is completed. With #22 needle, work pearl cotton embroidery.

3 Overcast bottom edges of sides and inside edges of top with adjacent colors. Whipstitch sides together with sail blue and white following graph, then Whipstitch sides to top with sail blue. ■

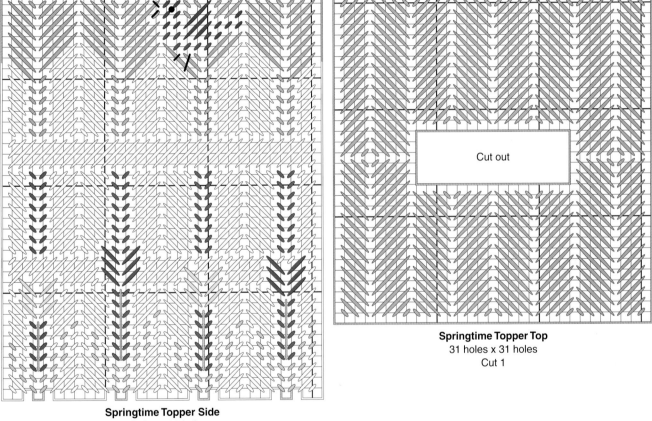

Springtime Topper Side
31 holes x 38 holes
Cut 4

Springtime Topper Top
31 holes x 31 holes
Cut 1

Tips & Techniques

When I know I am going to make the same project several times, I cut a master copy of the pattern pieces from a darker or brighter color of plastic canvas. It makes cutting the pattern pieces simpler and easier on the eyes.

—*Bonnie Dominguez, California*

I got tired of counting plastic canvas holes. From scraps, I cut pieces measuring 10 holes, 20 holes, 30 holes, etc. I lay these markers across the plastic canvas to help me count quickly and easily.

—*Charlett Haws, Kansas*

I save all my yarn scraps 2 inches and longer in a bag. When we take a trip, I take the bag along and stitch coasters in the Texas Lone Star pattern, using every little scrap. I usually complete the background in off-white.

—*Betty Werline, Texas*

To keep different colors of yarn separate and tangle-free for a "take-along" project, roll the colors in balls and store them all in the same large zipper-seal bag. Punch a separate small hole in the bag for each color, and thread the yarn end through to the outside. I can then pull out and cut off the desired length of the desired color, and nothing gets tangled. The project can even be slipped in the bag when stitching time is over.

—*Deb Arch, Illinois*

Life on the Farm

*Designed for country folk and country folk at heart,
this farmer's tissue topper is bursting with good old rural charm!*

Design by Mary T. Cosgrove

TAKE NOTE

Skill Level: Intermediate

Finished Size: 9½ inches W x 8 inches H x 4¾ inches D

YOU'LL NEED

- 2¼ sheets Uniek Quick-Count 7-count plastic canvas
- Uniek Needloft plastic canvas yarn as listed in color key
- Kreinik Heavy (#32) Braid as listed in color key
- #16 tapestry needle

INSTRUCTIONS

1 Cut plastic canvas according to graphs (this page and pages, 13 and 14).

2 Stitch pieces following graphs. When background stitching is completed, work white vertical Backstitches on barn doors. With black heavy braid Backstitches, outline farmer and work Straight Stitches and French Knots on horses.

3 Using black throughout, Overcast top edges of barn roof pieces, then Whipstitch together along side edges. Overcast silo roof.

4 Using white through step 7, with a Continental Stitch, Whipstitch inside barn wall between front and back pieces to bars indicated on front and back with blue line, making sure wrong side is facing barn side.

5 Whipstitch outside barn wall to side edges of barn, then Whipstitch bottom edges of roof to top edges of the barn's four walls.

6 Whipstitch silo wall to side edges of silo, then Whipstitch silo floor to bottom edges of silo and inside barn wall.

7 Overcast all remaining edges. ■

COLOR KEY

Plastic Canvas Yarn	Yards
■ Black #00	48
■ Christmas red #02	85
☐ Pink #07	1
☐ Straw #19	3
■ Royal #32	1
☐ White #41	18
■ Camel #43	2
✎ White #41 Backstitch	
Heavy (#32) Braid	
✎ Black #005HL Backstitch and Straight Stitch	
● Black #005HL French Knot	3

Color numbers given are for Uniek Needloft plastic canvas yarn and Kreinik Heavy (#32) Braid.

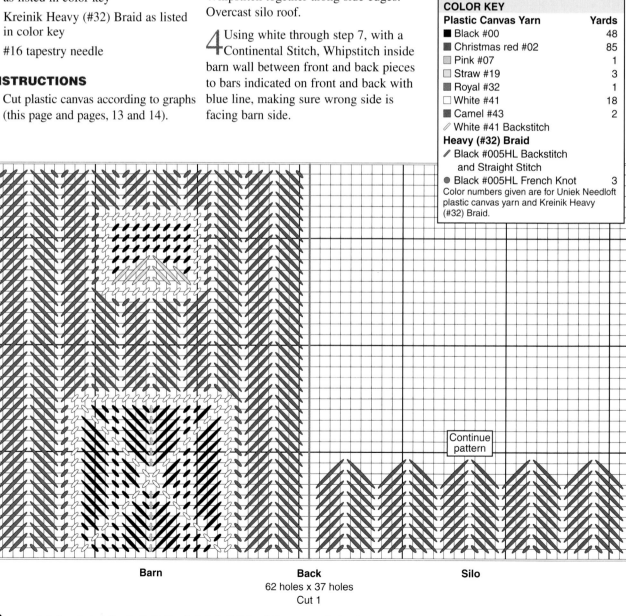

Continue pattern

Barn

Back
62 holes x 37 holes
Cut 1

Silo

Outside Barn Wall
31 holes x 37 holes
Cut 1

Silo Wall
31 holes x 37 holes
Cut 1

Continue pattern

Inside Barn Wall
31 holes x 37 holes
Cut 1

Continue pattern

Silo Floor
31 holes x 31 holes
Cut 1

Barn Roof
31 holes x 15 holes
Cut 4

Silo

Front
62 holes x 52 holes
Cut 1

Barn

Rosebud Gazebo

*Adorned with delicate, pink rosebuds, this enchanting gazebo
will discreetly cover a spare toilet tissue roll!*

Design by Lee Lindeman

TAKE NOTE

Skill Level: Beginner

Finished Size: 8¼ inches H x 8 inches in diameter

YOU'LL NEED

- ☐ 3 sheets 7-count plastic canvas
- ☐ Worsted weight yarn as listed in color key
- ☐ #16 tapestry needle
- ☐ 1¾-inch white pompom
- ☐ 10 (½-inch) pink ribbon roses
- ☐ 2 yards ¼-inch-wide pink satin ribbon
- ☐ Hot-glue gun

INSTRUCTIONS

1 Cut plastic canvas according to graphs.

2 Stitch pieces following graphs. Work base top as graphed. Reverse base bottom and work with pink Continental Stitches.

3 Overcast bushes with dark green. For gazebo walls, Overcast inside edges with medium green and top and bottom edges with white. For roof sections, Overcast bottom edges with medium green and top edges with white.

4 Place wrong sides of base pieces together matching edges. Whipstitch both inside edges and outside edges together with medium green.

5 Using white throughout, Whipstitch side edges of roof sections together. Whipstitch gazebo walls together.

6 Using photo as a guide through step 8, glue gazebo walls to base top along inside edges. Glue roof to top edges of gazebo walls, spreading out roof as necessary to fit. Glue bushes to corners of gazebo along base.

7 Glue pompom to top of roof. Glue one silk rose to each panel around base of pompom. Center and glue remaining roses above gazebo windows.

8 For roses on bushes, tie 30 knots in pink ribbon. Carefully cut knots from ribbon and glue six to each bush. ■

COLOR KEY	
Worsted Weight Yarn	**Yards**
☐ White	67
▨ Medium green	30
☐ Pink	12
■ Dark green	7

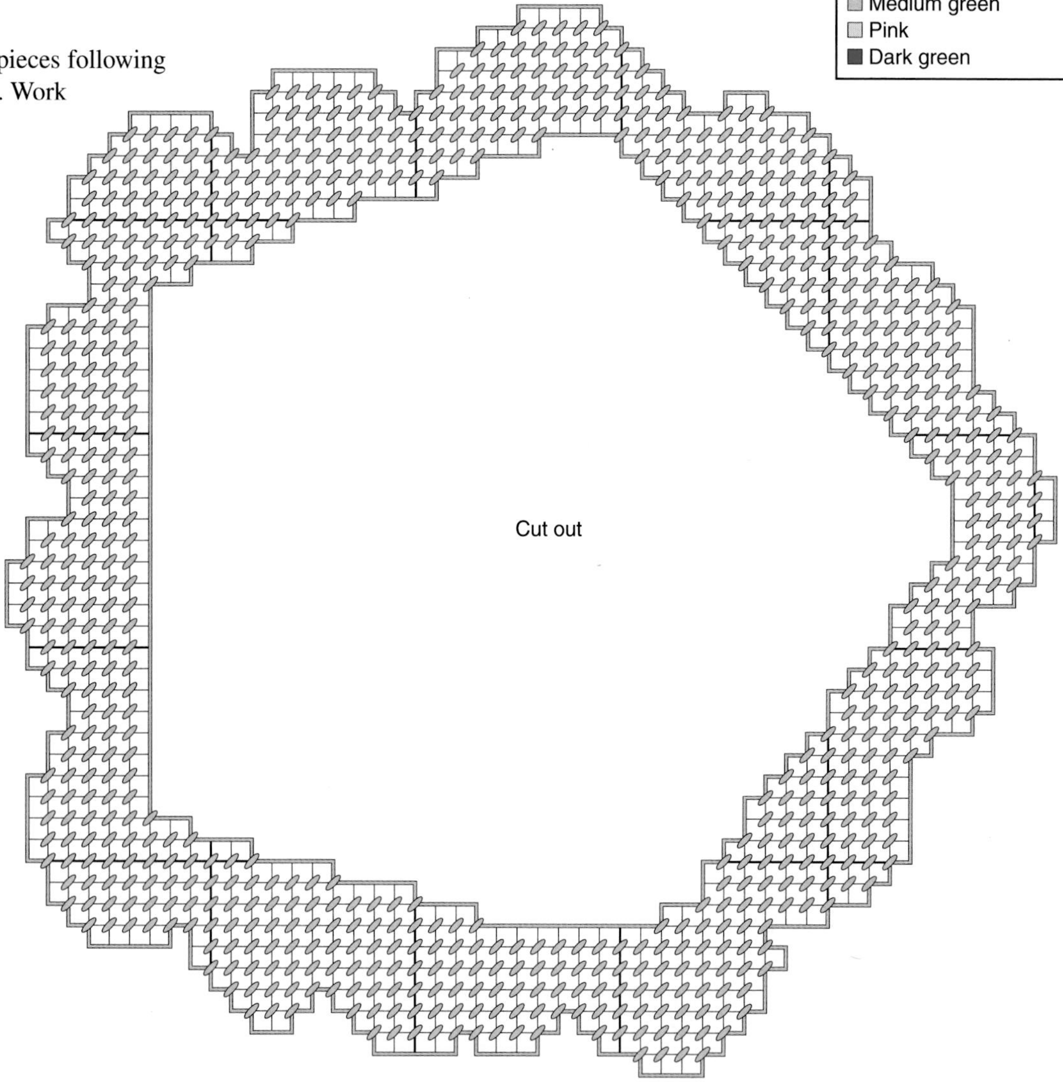

Gazebo Base Top & Bottom
51 holes x 50 holes
Cut 2
Stitch base top as graphed
Reverse base bottom and stitch
with pink Continental Stitches

Cut out

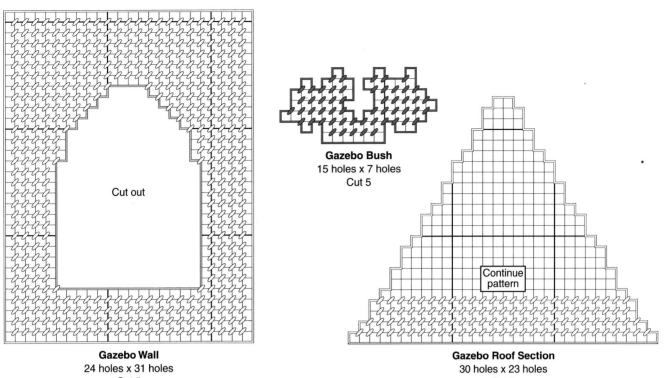

Gazebo Wall
24 holes x 31 holes
Cut 5

Gazebo Bush
15 holes x 7 holes
Cut 5

Continue pattern

Gazebo Roof Section
30 holes x 23 holes
Cut 5

Golden Anchors
Continued from page 7

Continued from page 7

COLOR KEY	
Worsted Weight Yarn	**Yards**
■ Scarlet #8933	16
□ White #8942	16
■ Navy #8965	45
Uncoded areas are navy #8965 Continental Stitches	
¹⁄₈-Inch Metallic Needlepoint Yarn	
□ Gold #PC1	16
∕ Gold #PC1 Backstitch and Straight Stitch	
¹⁄₁₆-Inch Metallic Needlepoint Yarn	
∕ Gold #PM51 Backstitch and Straight Stitch	2
○ Gold #PM51 French Knot	

Color numbers given are for Spinrite Bernat Berella "4" worsted weight yarn and Rainbow Gallery ¹⁄₈-inch-wide Plastic Canvas 7 Metallic Needlepoint Yarn and ¹⁄₁₆-inch-wide Plastic Canvas 10 Metallic Needlepoint Yarn.

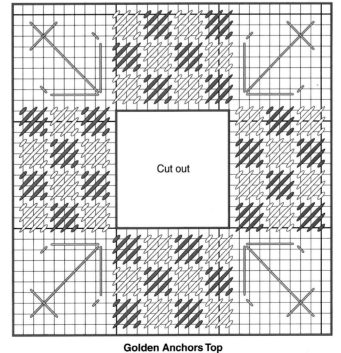

Golden Anchors Top
31 holes x 31 holes
Cut 1

Flowers 'n' Checks

*With bright blue stripes and checks bordering three sunny flowers,
this pretty tissue box cover will brighten up any spot in your home!*

Design by Nancy Marshall

TAKE NOTE

Skill Level: Beginner

Finished Size: Fits standard-size tissue box

YOU'LL NEED

☐ 1¼ sheets 7-count plastic canvas

☐ #16 tapestry needle

☐ Uniek Needloft plastic canvas yarn as listed in color key

INSTRUCTIONS

1 Cut plastic canvas according to graphs.

2 Stitch pieces following graphs, working uncoded areas on sides with white Continental Stitches.

3 Overcast inside edges on top and bottom edges on sides with white. Whipstitch long sides to short sides with white and royal following graphs, then Whipstitch sides to top with white. ▪

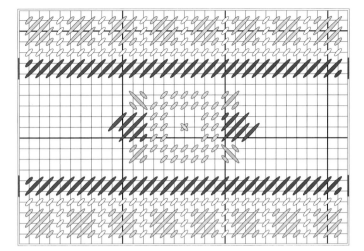

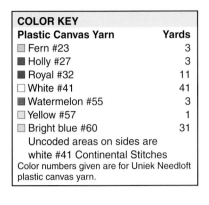

COLOR KEY

Plastic Canvas Yarn	Yards
☐ Fern #23	3
■ Holly #27	3
■ Royal #32	11
☐ White #41	41
■ Watermelon #55	3
☐ Yellow #57	1
☐ Bright blue #60	31

Uncoded areas on sides are white #41 Continental Stitches
Color numbers given are for Uniek Needloft plastic canvas yarn.

Flowers 'n' Checks Short Side
32 holes x 22 holes
Cut 2

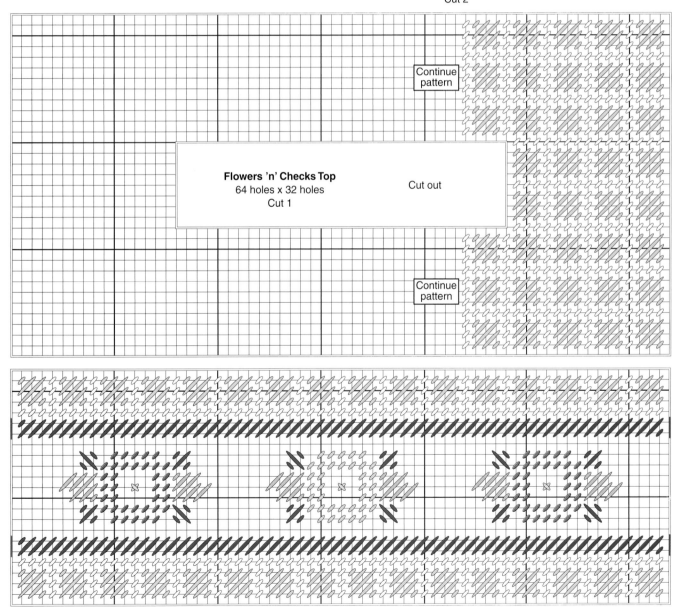

Continue pattern

Flowers 'n' Checks Top
64 holes x 32 holes
Cut 1

Cut out

Continue pattern

Flowers 'n' Checks Long Side
64 holes x 22 holes
Cut 2

Victorian Armoire

Add a decorative accent to your home with this artistic tissue box cover. Shaped like an armoire, the back of this cover is adorned with beautiful foxgloves.

Design by Janelle Giese

TAKE NOTE

Skill Level: Intermediate

Finished Size: 5½ inches W x 11½ inches H x 4 inches D

YOU'LL NEED

- 3 sheets Uniek Quick-Count black 7-count plastic canvas
- Lion Chenille Sensations acrylic yarn from Lion Brand Yarn Co. as listed in color key
- Uniek Needloft plastic canvas yarn as listed in color key
- Kreinik ⅛-inch Ribbon as listed in color key
- DMC 6-strand embroidery floss as listed in color key
- DMC #5 pearl cotton as listed in color key
- #16 tapestry needle
- ⅔ yard 2-inch-wide black fringe
- Aquarium gravel
- Thick white glue
- Straight pins

PROJECT NOTES

Work project in following order: ⅛-inch ribbon, plastic canvas yarn and chenille yarn.

Work with 1 yard lengths of chenille yarn.

INSTRUCTIONS

1 Cut plastic canvas according to graphs (this page and pages 22 and 24). Cut two 34-hole x 24-hole pieces for base and inner base, two 32-hole x 10-hole pieces for long lid lip pieces and two 22-hole x 10-hole pieces for short lid lip pieces. Base pieces and lid lip pieces will remain unstitched.

2 Stitch pieces following graphs and Project Notes, working uncoded areas with black chenille yarn Continental Stitches and leaving blue lines unstitched. Overcast inside edges on back with black.

3 When background stitching is completed, work black pearl cotton Backstitches. Using two strands embroidery floss, Cross Stitch shading on flowers.

4 Using black chenille yarn through step 6, Whipstitch front and back to sides. Overcast top edges. Slide unstitched inner base inside box and Continental Stitch to front, back and sides where indicated with blue lines.

5 Whipstitch unstitched base to bottom edge of armoire, filling base with aquarium gravel before closing.

6 Whipstitch long lid lip pieces to short lid lip pieces along short edges, then Continental Stitch to lid top where indicated with blue lines. Overcast lid top edges and bottom edges of lid lips.

7 Glue fringe around completed armoire 13 bars from bottom edge, using straight pins to hold in place until glue sets. ▨

COLOR KEY

Chenille Acrylic Yarn	Yards
▩ Madrid print #406	20
Uncoded areas are black #153 Continental Stitches	105
╱ Black #153 Overcasting and Whipstitching	
Plastic Canvas Yarn	
▩ Pink #07	2
▩ Tan #18	2
▢ Holly #27	1
▩ Forest #29	2
▢ Beige #40	1
▢ Orchid #44	2
▩ Purple #46	1
▨ Plum #59	2
⅛-Inch Ribbon	
▢ Antique gold #205C	23
#5 Pearl Cotton	
╱ Black #310 Backstitch and Straight Stitch	4
6-Strand Embroidery Floss	
✕ Very dark violet #550 Cross Stitch	1
✕ Dark drab brown #611 Cross Stitch	1
✕ Mauve #3687 Cross Stitch	1

Color numbers given are for Lion Brand Lion Chenille Sensations acrylic yarn, Uniek Needloft plastic canvas yarn, Kreinik ⅛-inch Ribbon and DMC #5 pearl cotton and 6-strand embroidery floss.

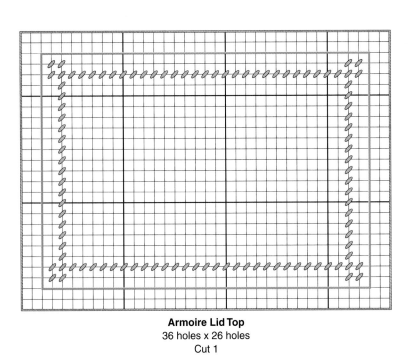

Armoire Lid Top
36 holes x 26 holes
Cut 1

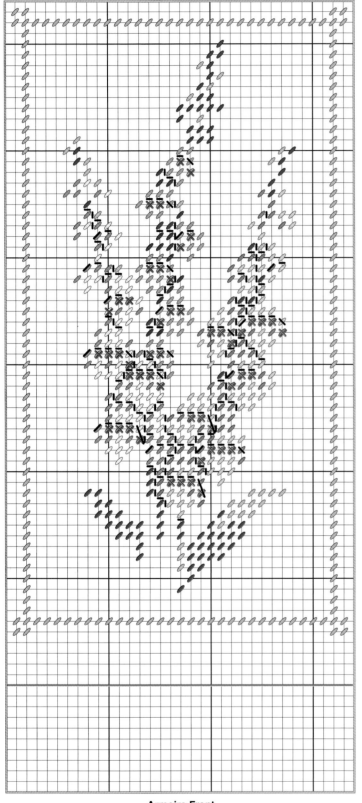

Armoire Front
34 holes x 74 holes
Cut 1

Armoire Side
24 holes x 74 holes
Cut 2

Graphs continued on page 24

Victorian Bouquet

A dainty bouquet of French Knots gives this lovely tissue box cover added texture and charm.

Design by Linda Wyszynski

TAKE NOTE

Skill Level: Beginner

Finished Size: Fits boutique-style tissue box

YOU'LL NEED

- □ 1½ sheets Uniek Quick-Count 7-count plastic canvas
- □ Coats & Clark Red Heart Super Saver worsted weight yarn Art. #300 as listed in color key
- □ Kreinik Heavy (#32) Braid as listed in color key
- □ Kreinik Very Fine (#4) Braid as listed in color key
- □ DMC #5 pearl cotton: 5 yards each medium lavender #210, light old gold #676, dark garnet #814, dark navy blue #823 and as listed in color key
- □ #18 tapestry needle
- □ 1¼ inch brass bee charm #4457 from Creative Beginnings
- □ Clear thread

INSTRUCTIONS

1 Cut plastic canvas according to graphs (page 24).

2 Stitch pieces following graphs, working uncoded areas with Aran Continental Stitches.

3 When background stitching is completed, use gold heavy (#32) braid to form a bow (Fig. 1) on each cover side over gold Continental Stitch bow. Use gold very fine (#4) braid to couch in place over Continental Stitches. Tie a knot in bow ends.

4 For top, Overcast inside edges with Aran, then work gold very fine (#4) braid Backstitches. Work Lazy Daisy Stitches for leaves with blue green pearl cotton.

5 Work French Knots on top as desired around Lazy Daisy Stitches with medium lavender, light old gold, dark garnet and dark navy blue pearl cotton, wrapping pearl cotton three times around needle. Make some knots looser and some tighter for different flower sizes.

6 Using photo as a guide for placement, work flowers on sides following step 5.

7 Using clear thread, attach bee to top where indicated on graph.

8 Using soft navy throughout, Overcast bottom edges of sides. Whipstitch sides together, then Whipstitch sides to top. ■

COLOR KEY	
Worsted Weight Yarn	**Yards**
■ Burgundy #376	32
■ Soft navy #387	28
■ Hunter green #389	25
Uncoded areas are Aran #313 Continental Stitches	20
⁄ Aran #313 Overcasting	
Heavy (#32) Braid	
□ Gold #002	10
Very Fine (#4) Braid	
⁄ Gold #002 Backstitch	6
#5 Pearl Cotton	
⬮ Blue green #502 Lazy Daisy	5
○ Attach bee	
Color numbers given are for Coats & Clark Red Heart Super Saver worsted weight yarn Art. E300, Kreinik Heavy (#32) Braid and Very Fine (#4) Braid and DMC #5 pearl cotton.	

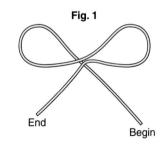

Fig. 1

End

Begin

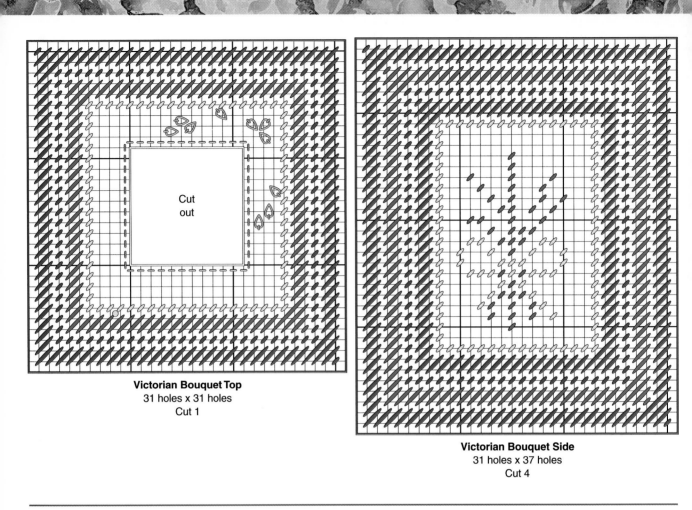

Victorian Bouquet Top
31 holes x 31 holes
Cut 1

Victorian Bouquet Side
31 holes x 37 holes
Cut 4

Victorian Armoire
Continued from page 22

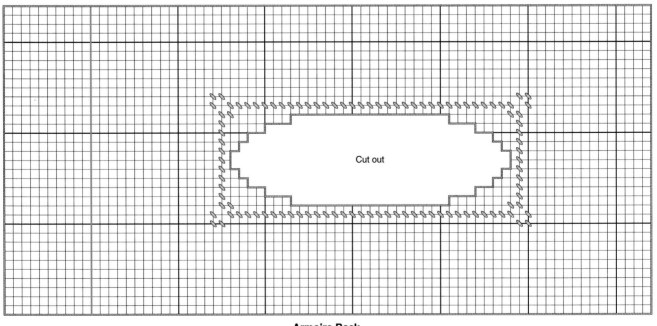

Armoire Back
34 holes x 74 holes
Cut 1

Hearts & Lace

Dress up your bathroom with this pair of tissue paper covers, one for your facial tissue and another for toilet tissue.

Design by Angie Arickx

TAKE NOTE

Skill Level: Beginner

Finished Size: Fits boutique-style tissue box and regular size roll bathroom tissue

YOU'LL NEED

- □ 2½ sheets 7-count plastic canvas
- □ Uniek Needloft plastic canvas yarn as listed in color key
- □ #16 tapestry needle

INSTRUCTIONS

1 Following graphs (page 30), cut four sides for each cover from plastic canvas. Leave center area intact on toilet tissue cover top. Cut out center hole on tissue box cover top only, making blue lines the edge lines.

2 Stitch pieces following graphs, working uncoded areas with white Continental Stitches.

3 Using white throughout, Overcast inside edges of tissue box cover top and bottom edges of all sides. For each cover, Whipstitch four sides together, then Whipstitch top to sides. ▧

COLOR KEY	
Plastic Canvas Yarn	**Yards**
■ Lavender #05	57
□ Pink #07	64
Uncoded areas are white #41	
Continental Stitches	85
⁄ White #41 Overcasting and Whipstitching	
Color numbers given are for Uniek Needloft plastic canvas yarn.	

Graphs on page 30

Granny Squares Tissue Topper

Inspired by the traditional granny square motif used in crochet, this tissue box cover can be worked in any colors to match your decor.

Design by Robin Howard-Will

TAKE NOTE

Skill Level: Beginner

Finished Size: Fits boutique-style tissue box

YOU'LL NEED

□ 3 sheets light brown 7-count plastic canvas

□ Coats & Clark Super Saver worsted weight yarn Art. E301 as listed in color key

□ #16 tapestry needle

INSTRUCTIONS

1 Cut and stitch plastic canvas according to graphs.

2 With hunter green, Whipstitch sides together, then Whipstitch sides to top. Overcast bottom edges. Do not Overcast inside edges of top. ∎

Top Edge

COLOR KEY

Plastic Canvas Yarn	Yards
☐ Warm brown #336	28
■ Claret #378	4
■ Hunter green #389	52

Color numbers given are for Coats & Clark Red Heart Super Saver worsted weight yarn Art. E301.

Granny Squares Side
47 holes x 47 holes
Cut 4

Cut out

Granny Squares Top
43 holes x 43 holes
Cut 1

King's Castle

Unleash your child's imagination with this medieval tissue topper!

Design by Janelle Giese

TAKE NOTE

Skill Level: Intermediate

Finished Size: $4\frac{5}{8}$ inches W x $7\frac{3}{8}$ inches H x $5\frac{3}{8}$ inches D

YOU'LL NEED

☐ 2 sheets 7-count plastic canvas

☐ Chenille acrylic yarn as listed in color key

☐ Uniek Needloft plastic canvas yarn as listed in color key

☐ DMC #3 pearl cotton as listed in color key

☐ #16 tapestry needle

INSTRUCTIONS

1 Cut plastic canvas according to graphs (this page and page 30). Do not stitch flagpole.

2 Stitch pieces following graphs. Do not stitch uncoded areas shaded with pale yellow. Work all remaining uncoded areas with silver Continental Stitches, leaving bars with blue lines unstitched.

3 When background stitching is completed, work black pearl cotton Backstitches and Straight Stitches.

4 Overcast flagpole with sandstone where shown on graph. With burgundy, Overcast flag and Whipstitch edges from dot to dot to remaining edges of flagpole. With sandstone, tack bottom edge of flagpole to roof where indicated on graph.

5 Using silver through step 9, Overcast edges of opening in roof. Overcast bottom edges of sandpile from dot to dot. Overcast top and inside edges of roof extensions on castle front and sides, but do not Overcast edges between extensions or outside edges of extensions.

6 With a Continental Stitch, Whipstitch right edge of castle turret to castle front along vertical bar indicated with blue line, then Whipstitch to roof extension above blue line.

7 Whipstitch three castle side pieces together, forming one long piece. Whipstitch sides to front and to turret, working through all three thicknesses on left side of front. *Note: Turret will curve out.*

8 Slide roof into top of castle and Whipstitch in place to bars indicated with blue lines and to edges between roof extensions.

9 With a Continental Stitch, Whipstitch sandpile to turret and front where indicated with blue lines. ■

COLOR KEY

Chenille Acrylic Yarn	Yards
✏ Silver Overcasting and Whipstitching	88
Plastic Canvas Yarn	
■ Black #00	6
■ Burgundy #03	2
■ Gray #38	2
✏ Sandstone #16 Overcasting	1
#3 Pearl Cotton	
✏ Black #310 Backstitch and Straight Stitch	4
○ Attach flagpole	

Color numbers given are for Uniek Needloft plastic canvas yarn and DMC #3 pearl cotton.

Flag
7 holes x 5 holes
Cut 1

Flagpole
1 hole x 10 holes
Cut 1
Do not stitch

Sandpile
25 holes x 6 holes
Cut 1

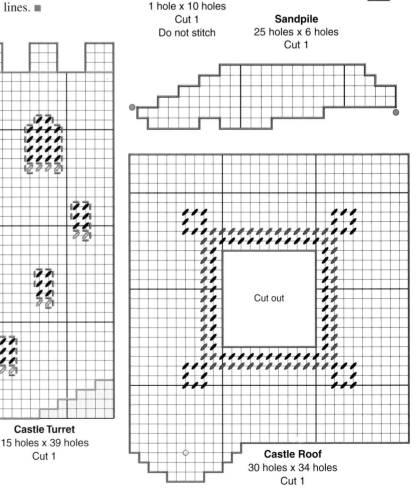

Castle Turret
15 holes x 39 holes
Cut 1

Cut out

Castle Roof
30 holes x 34 holes
Cut 1

Graphs continued on page 30

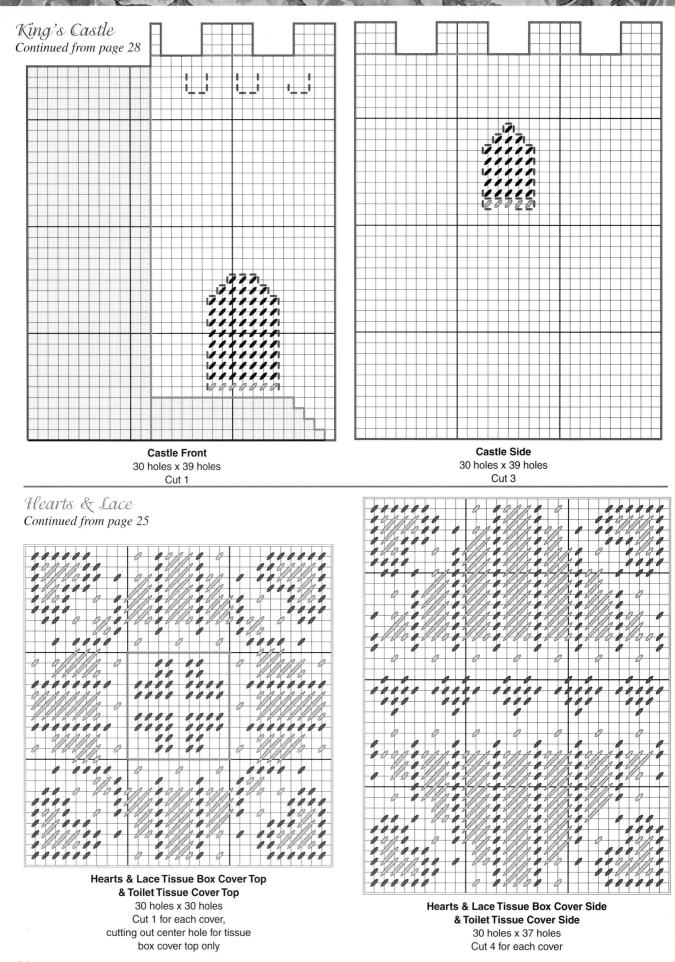

King's Castle
Continued from page 28

Castle Front
30 holes x 39 holes
Cut 1

Castle Side
30 holes x 39 holes
Cut 3

Hearts & Lace
Continued from page 25

Hearts & Lace Tissue Box Cover Top
& Toilet Tissue Cover Top
30 holes x 30 holes
Cut 1 for each cover,
cutting out center hole for tissue
box cover top only

Hearts & Lace Tissue Box Cover Side
& Toilet Tissue Cover Side
30 holes x 37 holes
Cut 4 for each cover

Creative Coasters

With this collection of fun and fancy coasters, you can
add a touch of your own personality and style to the
simple task of protecting your furniture from water rings!

Down-on-the-Farm Fun

Country folks will love using this whimsical coaster set featuring five friendly animals and a red barn storage case!
Photo on page 31.

Designs by Lee Lindeman

TAKE NOTE

Skill Level: Intermediate

Finished Size:

Lamb Coaster: $3\frac{7}{8}$ inches W x $3\frac{7}{8}$ inches L

Turkey Coaster: $3\frac{7}{8}$ inches W x $3\frac{7}{8}$ inches L

Duck Coaster: $3\frac{3}{4}$ inches W x $4\frac{1}{2}$ inches L including tail feathers

Rooster Coaster: $4\frac{3}{4}$ inches W x $4\frac{1}{4}$ inches L

Pig Coaster: $4\frac{1}{2}$ inches W x $3\frac{3}{4}$ inches L including tail

Red Barn Holder: $6\frac{1}{2}$ inches W x $5\frac{1}{2}$ inches H x $7\frac{1}{4}$ inches D

YOU'LL NEED

- 4 sheets 7-count plastic canvas
- Worsted weight yarn: 3 yards tan and as listed in color key
- Natural raffia as listed in color key
- 6-strand embroidery floss as listed in color key
- #16 tapestry needle
- 16 (3mm) black beads
- Sewing needle and black sewing thread
- Brown marker
- 2 sheets black felt
- Small amount red felt
- Small amount medium pink felt
- Small amount yellow craft foam
- Small amount of gold lamé fabric
- Pencil
- Miniature bucket or ½-inch cork (optional)
- Gray and black acrylic craft paint (optional)
- Paintbrush (optional)
- 2 inches thin wire (optional)
- Tacky craft glue
- Hot-glue gun

PROJECT NOTE

Use hot-glue gun for all gluing unless otherwise stated.

BARNYARD CUTTING & STITCHING

1 Cut barn pieces, horse heads, bushes and base pieces from plastic canvas according to graphs (pages 33, 34 and 35). Cut one 29-hole x 29-hole piece for barn floor. Barn floor will remain unstitched.

2 Using barn front, back, sides, floor and roof sections as templates, cut black felt slightly smaller than each piece. Set aside. Using barn doors as templates, cut red felt slightly smaller than each door. Set aside.

3 For horses' ears, cut four narrow triangles about ½ inch high from black felt. Set aside.

4 Stitch pieces following graphs, working uncoded area on turkey with country red Continental Stitches and uncoded area on barn pieces with red Continental Stitches. Reverse two horse heads before stitching. Reverse base bottom before stitching and work entirely with green Continental Stitches.

5 Work natural raffia Turkey Loop Stitches in bottoms of haymow windows as desired on barn front and back. In door opening on barn front, carefully cut part of the natural raffia stitching on the left side of straw, being careful not to cut through the entire Continental Stitch.

6 Overcast barn doors with white and bushes with green.

7 Sew one bead to each horse head with sewing needle and black sewing thread where indicated on graph.

RED BARN ASSEMBLY

1 For lining, center and glue felt to corresponding pieces, allowing room along edges for Overcasting and Whipstitching.

2 With red, Whipstitch barn front and back to barn sides. Whipstitch front, back and sides to floor with red and dark gray following graphs. Overcast top edges of barn with red.

3 With white, Whipstitch roof sections together along long edges, forming a four-section strip. Overcast around all four sections.

4 Using photo as a guide, center and glue two roof sections to roof edges on one half of barn, leaving other side open for storing coasters. Glue left edge of one barn door to left side of barn door opening and right edge of remaining door to right side of barn door opening.

BARNYARD ASSEMBLY

1 Use photo as a guide throughout assembly. Matching edges and using green, Whipstitch wrong sides of base top and bottom together.

2 Glue barn to base top so that barn door is along edge of gray and green stitching.

3 Matching edges and using rust, Whipstitch wrong sides of two horse heads together from front of head to just below mouth. Using black floss, Straight Stitch mouth over edge. Complete Whipstitching.

4 For horse's mane, stitch ¼-inch-long loops with medium brown yarn through rust Whipstitching where indicated on graph from orange dot to orange dot.

5 For nose, using brown marker, color a small area of yarn on edge where indicated.

6 Repeat steps 3–5 with remaining horse head pieces. For ears, fold bottom ends of each black felt triangle together and secure with a dot of glue, then glue to horse heads where indicated on graph with blue dot.

7 Glue back edge of one horse to window on one barn side. Repeat with remaining horse, gluing to window on barn back. Glue one bush to each side of barn.

8 *Optional:* If using miniature bucket, glue bucket to base on right side of barn door.

9 *Optional:* If using cork for bucket, paint cork sides and a rim around top of cork with gray acrylic craft paint. Paint center area inside gray rim on top with black. Allow to dry. Bend wire in shape of handle; insert ends into cork, trimming to desired size. Glue to base as in step 8.

COASTER CUTTING & STITCHING

1 Cut two of each coaster following graphs (pages 34 and 35).

2 Using patterns given, cut two bells from gold lamé fabric and two pig ears from dark pink felt. Set aside.

3 Continental Stitch pieces following graphs, reversing one of each coaster before stitching. Work black floss Backstitches when background stitching is completed.

4 Attach beads for eyes where indicated with sewing needle and black sewing thread.

5 With red yarn, stitch a ³⁄₈-inch loop for wattle on rooster pieces where indicated on graph.

6 Whipstitch wrong sides of corresponding coasters together following graphs.

COASTER FINISHING

1 For lamb, cut two 6-inch lengths of white yarn and thread through hole indicated for tail. Separate lengths into one 3 ply and two 2 ply strands. Braid tail and tie off, separating strands at end, making tail 1 inch long. Center and glue one gold lamé bell under face on each side.

2 For turkey, cut two narrow ½-inch-long triangles from yellow craft foam for beak. Glue pieces together, then glue to front edge of turkey where indicated on graph. Cut a narrow ½-inch-long strip from red felt and glue over top and down one side of beak.

3 For pig, cut a 4-inch length of medium pink yarn. Moisten yarn with tacky glue and wrap around pencil. Allow to dry thoroughly, then remove from pencil and glue to pig where indicated on graph. Glue one dark pink felt pig ear to each side of pig where indicated on graph with blue dot.

4 For duck, stitch ⁵⁄₈-inch-long loops with white yarn through Whipstitching on tail where indicated on graph from dot to dot.

5 For rooster, cut two narrow ½-inch-long triangles from yellow craft foam for beak. Glue pieces together, then glue to front edge of rooster where indicated on graph. ▪

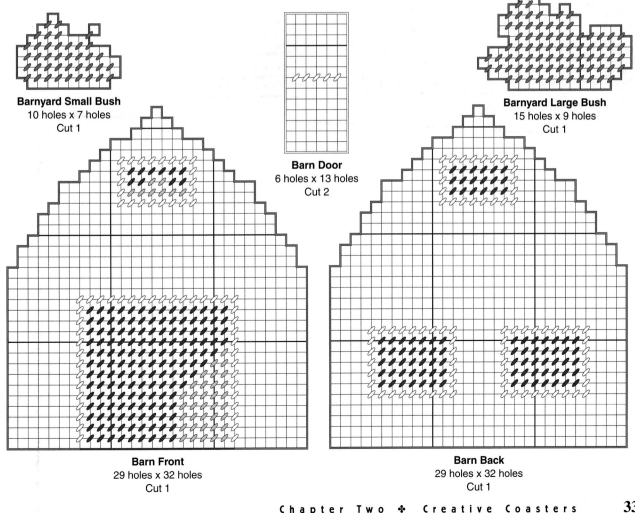

Barnyard Small Bush
10 holes x 7 holes
Cut 1

Barn Door
6 holes x 13 holes
Cut 2

Barnyard Large Bush
15 holes x 9 holes
Cut 1

Barn Front
29 holes x 32 holes
Cut 1

Barn Back
29 holes x 32 holes
Cut 1

COLOR KEY

Plastic Canvas Yarn	Yards
■ Green	95
□ White	55
■ Black	55
▨ Medium pink	27
▢ Off-white	18
▨ Medium brown	11
▨ Dark gray	11
■ Rust	8
▨ Light gray	5
▢ Yellow	4
▨ Bright red	4
▨ Orange	4
▨ Dark pink	2
Uncoded areas on barn are red Continental Stitches	69
Uncoded area on turkey coaster is country red Continental Stitches	6
⁄ Red Overcasting and Whipstitching	
⁄ Country red Whipstitching	
Raffia	
▨ Natural	4
6-Strand Embroidery Floss	
⁄ Black Backstitch	7
● Attach black bead	
● Attach tail	

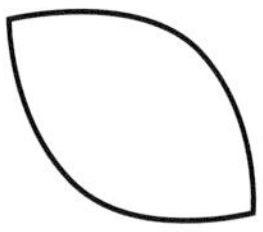

Pig Ear Pattern
Cut 2 from medium pink felt

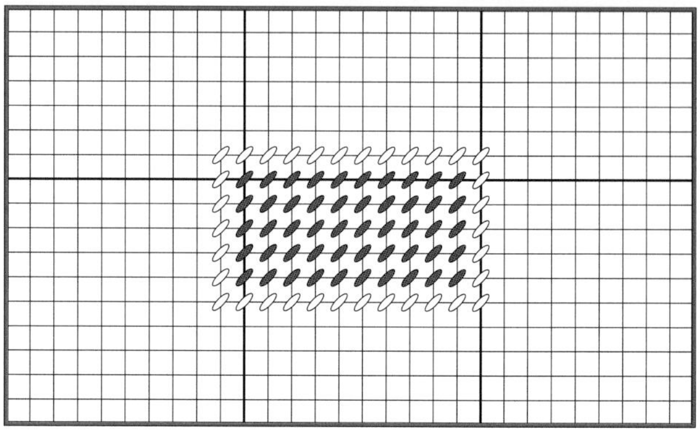

Barn Side
29 holes x 17 holes
Cut 2

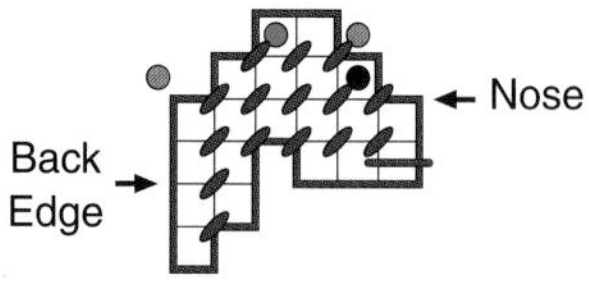

Horse Head
6 holes x 6 holes
Cut 4, reverse 2

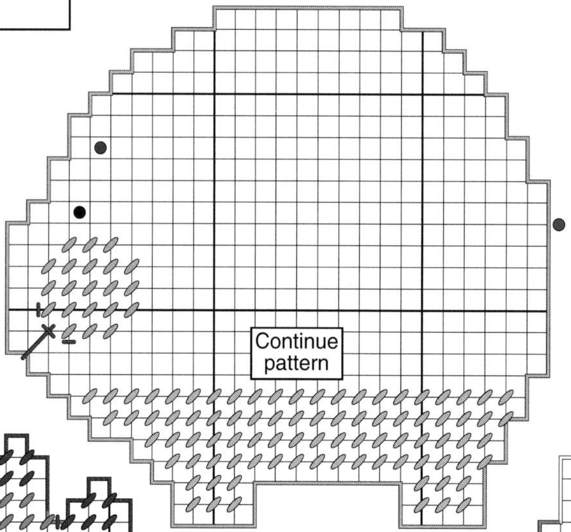

Back Edge
← Nose

Pig Coaster
26 holes x 24 holes
Cut 2, reverse 1

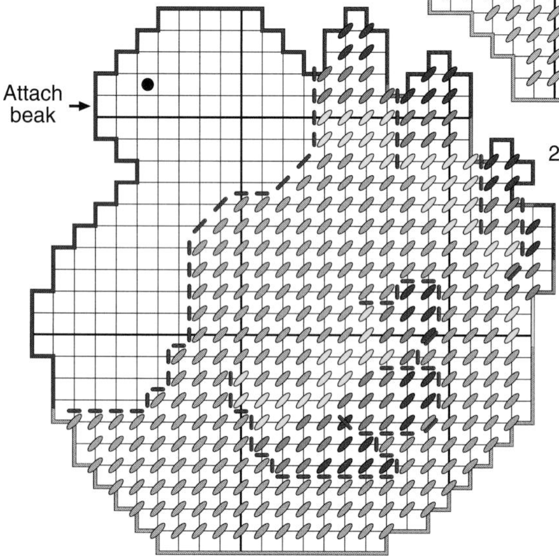

Continue pattern

Turkey Coaster
25 holes x 25 holes
Cut 2, reverse 1

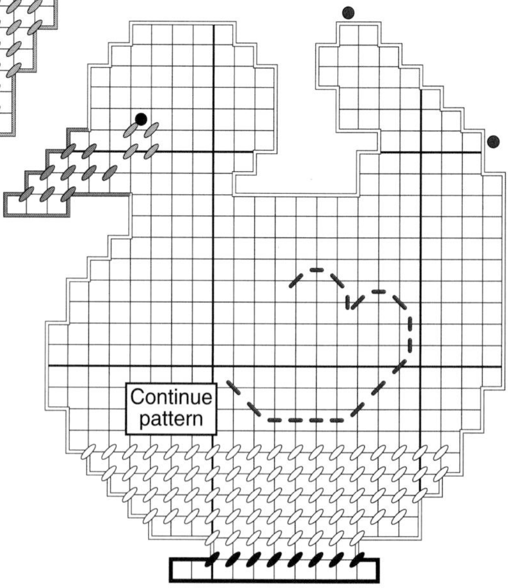

Attach beak →

Duck Coaster
24 holes x 26 holes
Cut 2, reverse 1

Continue pattern

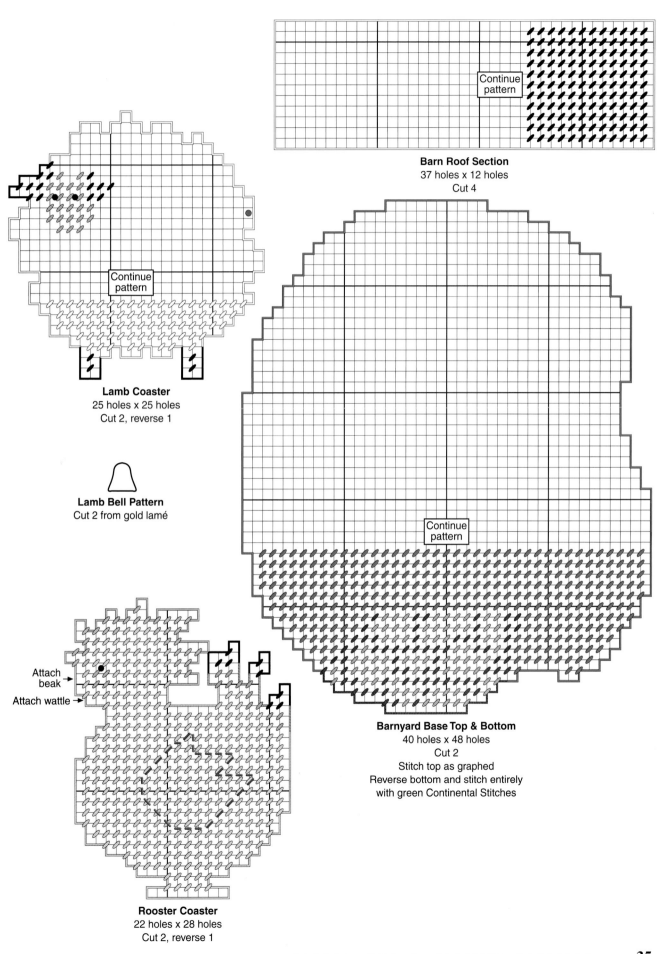

Barn Roof Section
37 holes x 12 holes
Cut 4

Lamb Coaster
25 holes x 25 holes
Cut 2, reverse 1

Continue pattern

Lamb Bell Pattern
Cut 2 from gold lamé

Continue pattern

Attach beak →

Attach wattle →

Barnyard Base Top & Bottom
40 holes x 48 holes
Cut 2
Stitch top as graphed
Reverse bottom and stitch entirely
with green Continental Stitches

Rooster Coaster
22 holes x 28 holes
Cut 2, reverse 1

Grand Slam Coasters

*Hit a grand slam with your baseball-loving family when you
stitch up this set of coasters with a bat holder!*

Design by Ruby Thacker

TAKE NOTE

Skill Level: Beginner

Finished Size:

Coasters: 3⅞ inches in diameter

Holder: 4¼ inches W x 4⅝ inches H
x 1¼ inches D

YOU'LL NEED

☐ 1 sheet 7-count plastic canvas

☐ Uniek Needloft plastic canvas yarn
as listed in color key

☐ #16 tapestry needle

INSTRUCTIONS

1 Cut plastic canvas according to
graphs (pages 38).

2 Stitch pieces following graphs.
When background stitching is completed, work red Backstitches on baseball coasters and white Straight Stitches on holder back.

3 Using Christmas green throughout,
Whipstitch wrong sides of holder
sides to wrong side of holder bottom
along short edges, forming one long
strip. Whipstitch wrong side of strip, to
right side of holder back along side and
bottom edges. Overcast all remaining
holder edges.

4 Overcast coasters with white and
bats with camel.

5 Using photo as a guide, crisscross
bats, then glue together and to edges
of holder sides and bottom. ■

Graphs continued on page 38

Country Cottage

Stitch up a charming country cottage surrounded by a white picket fence to make a delightful coaster set!

Design by Angie Arickx

TAKE NOTE

Skill Level: Beginner

Finished Size

Coasters: 4⅛ inches W x 3⅝ inches L

Coaster Holder: 4 inches W x 1½ inches H x 1½ inches D

YOU'LL NEED

☐ 1 sheet 7-count plastic canvas

☐ #16 tapestry needle

☐ Uniek Needloft plastic canvas yarn as listed in color key

INSTRUCTIONS

1 Cut plastic canvas according to graphs (pages 38). Cut one 25-hole x 9-hole piece for holder bottom. Holder bottom will remain unstitched.

2 Stitch coasters following graph, working uncoded areas with bright blue Continental stitches. When background stitching is completed, work watermelon French Knots. Overcast following graph.

3 With white, stitch and Overcast fence posts and rails on holder front, back and sides following graphs, but do not Overcast side edges. Overcast top edges of grass between fence posts with fern.

4 Whipstitch fence front and back to sides with white, then Whipstitch front, back and sides to unstitched bottom. ▨

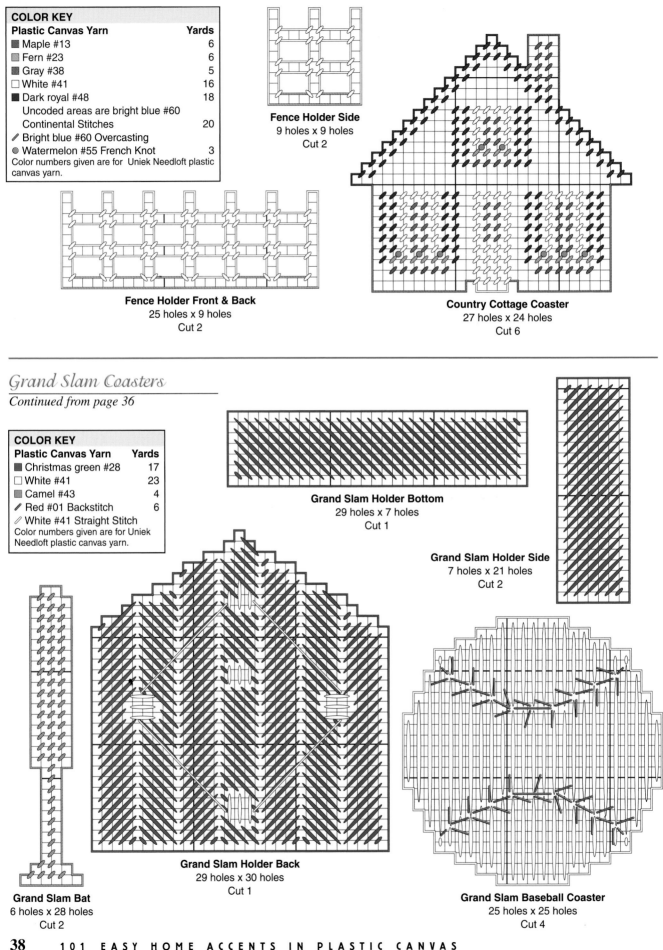

COLOR KEY

Plastic Canvas Yarn	Yards
■ Maple #13	6
■ Fern #23	6
■ Gray #38	5
□ White #41	16
■ Dark royal #48	18
Uncoded areas are bright blue #60	
Continental Stitches	20
⁄ Bright blue #60 Overcasting	
● Watermelon #55 French Knot	3
Color numbers given are for Uniek Needloft plastic canvas yarn.	

Fence Holder Side
9 holes x 9 holes
Cut 2

Fence Holder Front & Back
25 holes x 9 holes
Cut 2

Country Cottage Coaster
27 holes x 24 holes
Cut 6

Grand Slam Coasters

Continued from page 36

COLOR KEY

Plastic Canvas Yarn	Yards
■ Christmas green #28	17
□ White #41	23
■ Camel #43	4
⁄ Red #01 Backstitch	6
⁄ White #41 Straight Stitch	
Color numbers given are for Uniek Needloft plastic canvas yarn.	

Grand Slam Holder Bottom
29 holes x 7 holes
Cut 1

Grand Slam Holder Side
7 holes x 21 holes
Cut 2

Grand Slam Holder Back
29 holes x 30 holes
Cut 1

Grand Slam Bat
6 holes x 28 holes
Cut 2

Grand Slam Baseball Coaster
25 holes x 25 holes
Cut 4

Strawberry Patch

Stitch a basket of strawberries to enjoy during every season of the year!

Design by Angie Arickx

TAKE NOTE

Skill Level: Beginner

Finished Size:

Coasters: 3⅜ inches W x 3⅝ inches L

Coaster Holder: 3⅞ inches W x 2 inches H x 1⅛ inches D

YOU'LL NEED

- ☐ 1 sheet 7-count plastic canvas
- ☐ Uniek Needloft plastic canvas yarn as listed in color key
- ☐ #16 tapestry needle

INSTRUCTIONS

1 Cut plastic canvas according to graphs. Cut one 25-hole x 7-hole piece from plastic canvas for holder bottom. Holder bottom will remain unstitched.

2 Stitch pieces following graphs, working uncoded areas on strawberry coasters with Christmas red Continental Stitches and uncoded areas on holder pieces with cinnamon Continental Stitches.

3 Overcast strawberries with Christmas red and holly following graph. Using cinnamon throughout, Overcast top edges of holder front, back and sides, then Whipstitch front, back and sides to unstitched bottom. ■

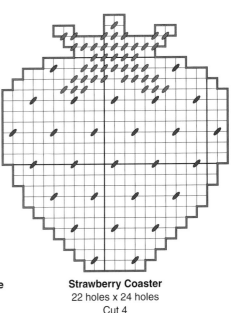

COLOR KEY	
Plastic Canvas Yarn	**Yards**
■ Black #13	2
■ Cinnamon #14	13
▨ Gold #17	13
■ Holly #27	5
Uncoded areas on coaster are Christmas red #02 Continental Stitches	26
Uncoded areas on holder pieces are cinnamon #14 Continental Stitches	
✎ Christmas red #02 Overcasting	
Color numbers given are for Uniek Needloft plastic canvas yarn.	

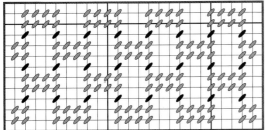

Strawberry Patch Holder Front & Back
25 holes x 12 holes
Cut 2

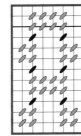

Strawberry Patch Holder Side
7 holes x 12 holes
Cut 2

Strawberry Coaster
22 holes x 24 holes
Cut 4

Ice Castle

Even your youngsters will remember to use coasters with this enchanting set in your family room!

Design by Celia Lange Designs

TAKE NOTE

Skill Level: Beginner

Finished Size:

Coasters: 4½ inches in diameter

Holder: 4 inches W x 3⅝ inches H x 2⅛ inches D

YOU'LL NEED

- ☐ 4 (4½ inch) plastic canvas radial circles by Darice
- ☐ ½ sheet 7-count plastic canvas
- ☐ Darice metallic cord as listed in color key
- ☐ Darice Bright Jewels metallic cord as listed in color key
- ☐ Darice Bright Pearls pearlized metallic cord as listed in color key
- ☐ 1 sheet purple Fun Foam craft foam by Westrim Crafts
- ☐ 4 (10mm) dark amethyst square #X640-002 faceted stones from The Beadery
- ☐ 6 (10mm x 14mm) dark sapphire octagon #X674-020 faceted stones from The Beadery
- ☐ Hot-glue gun

INSTRUCTIONS

1 Cut plastic canvas according to graphs. Cut one 26-hole x 11-hole piece for holder bottom. Do not cut plastic canvas radial circles.

2 Continental Stitch holder bottom with white/silver. Stitch remaining pieces following graphs.

3 Overcast coasters with blue/silver. Overcast castle front and back with white pearlized metallic cord. Overcast portcullis pieces with purple and silver following graphs, then work purple Backstitches.

4 Using white/silver throughout, Whipstitch holder front, back and sides together, then Whipstitch front, back and sides to bottom. Overcast top edges.

5 Using coasters as templates, cut circles from craft foam; glue to backs of coasters.

6 Using photo as a guide through step 7, place castle front inside holder, then center and glue right side of castle front to holder front. Repeat with castle back and holder back. Center and glue one portcullis to castle front and one to castle back, making sure bottom edges are even.

7 Glue two dark amethyst stones each to castle front and back. Glue two dark sapphire stones each to holder front and back. Center and glue remaining two dark sapphire stones to holder sides. ▪

COLOR KEY

Metallic Cord	Yards
■ White/silver #34021-112	18
■ Purple/silver #34021-113	20
■ Blue/silver 34021-115	20
■ Christmas green/silver #34021-407	20
☐ Silver #3411-02	2
■ Green #3411-05	1
■ Royal #3411-06	1
■ Purple #3411-07	3
╱ Puple Backstitch #3411-07	
╱ Blue/silver Backstitch #34021-115	
Pearlized Metallic Cord	
╱ White #3410-01 Overcasting	14
Uncoded area is white #3410-01 Continental Stitches	

Color numbers given are for Darice Metallic cord, Bright Jewels metallic cord and Bright Pearls pearlized metallic cord.

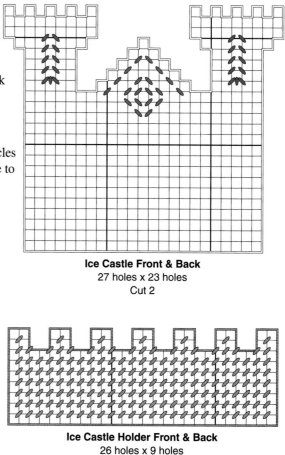

Ice Castle Front & Back
27 holes x 23 holes
Cut 2

Ice Castle Holder Front & Back
26 holes x 9 holes
Cut 2

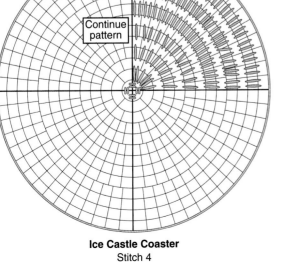

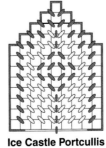

Ice Castle Coaster
Stitch 4

Ice Castle Portcullis
9 holes x 12 holes
Cut 2

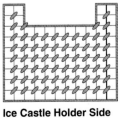

Ice Castle Holder Side
11 holes x 9 holes
Cut 2

Summertime Stitching

All your favorite summertime motifs come together in this bright-and-bold coaster set!

Designs by Robin Howard-Will

TAKE NOTE

Skill Level: Beginner

Finished Size:

    Coasters: Approximately 4⅝ inches square

    Coaster Holder: 4⅞ inches W x 6¼ inches H x 4⅞ inches D

YOU'LL NEED

- ☐ 3 sheets 7-count plastic canvas
- ☐ Darice Nylon Plus plastic canvas yarn as listed in color key
- ☐ #16 tapestry needle
- ☐ 3 yards ½-inch-wide gathered white lace
- ☐ Hot-glue gun or craft glue

INSTRUCTIONS

1 Cut plastic canvas according to graphs (pages 43 and 46). Cut one 31-hole x 31-hole piece for basket bottom. Basket bottom and six coaster pieces will remain unstitched.

2 Stitch remaining pieces following graphs, working uncoded areas with white Continental Stitches.

3 When background stitching is completed, work yellow Straight Stitches for sun's rays on sun coaster and black Straight Stitches for letters on basket sides.

4 Place wrong sides of basket handle together and Whipstitch around flower with purple. Overcast handle sides with white. Do not Overcast bottom edges of handles at this time.

5 Using white throughout, Whipstitch basket front and back to basket sides, then Whipstitch unstitched bottom to front, back and sides. Overcast top edges of basket, Whipstitching bottom edges of handles to front and back between dots while Overcasting.

6 Following graphs, Whipstitch unstitched coasters to back of stitched coasters.

7 Cut gathered lace into six 18-inch lengths. Glue one length of lace to back of each coaster around outside edges. ▨

COLOR KEY

Plastic Canvas Yarn	Yards
☐ White #01	68
■ Black #02	9
▤ Royal blue #09	16
▥ Burnt orange #17	11
■ Christmas red #19	12
■ Purple #21	16
▦ Lemon #25	3
☐ Yellow #26	16
■ Holly green #31	12
▦ Watermelon #54	2
▦ Fern #57	1
Uncoded areas are white #01 Continental Stitches	
╱ Black #02 Straight Stitch	
╱ Yellow #26 Straight Stitch	
Color numbers given are for Darice Nylon Plus plastic canvas yarn.	

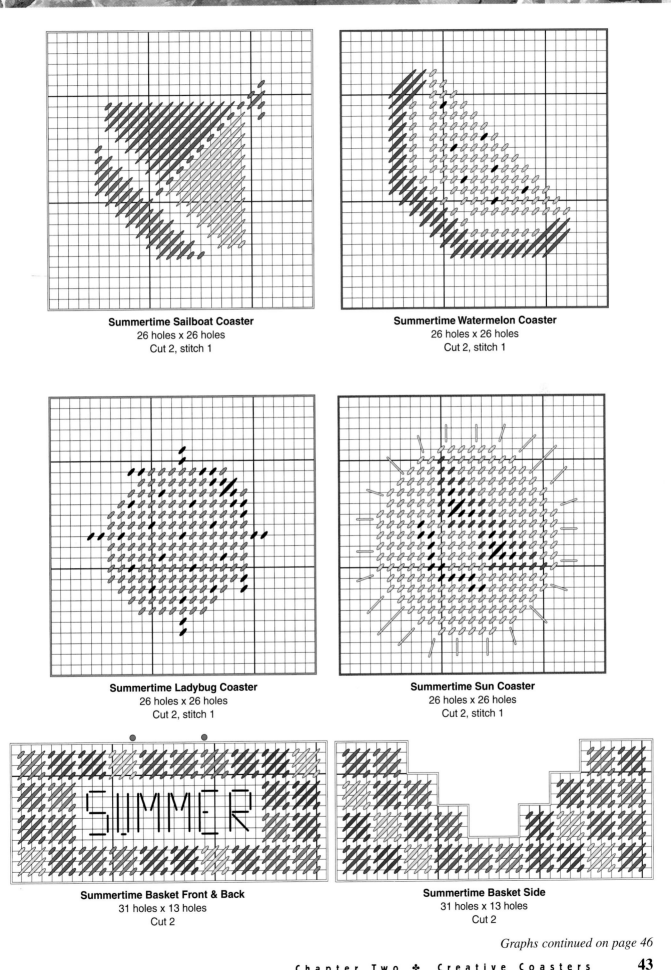

Summertime Sailboat Coaster
26 holes x 26 holes
Cut 2, stitch 1

Summertime Watermelon Coaster
26 holes x 26 holes
Cut 2, stitch 1

Summertime Ladybug Coaster
26 holes x 26 holes
Cut 2, stitch 1

Summertime Sun Coaster
26 holes x 26 holes
Cut 2, stitch 1

Summertime Basket Front & Back
31 holes x 13 holes
Cut 2

Summertime Basket Side
31 holes x 13 holes
Cut 2

Graphs continued on page 46

Classic Car Coasters

Reminisce about those days gone by with this set of classic car coasters with a scenic holder.

Design by Judy Collishaw

TAKE NOTE

Skill Level: Beginner

Finished Size

Coasters: 4¼ inches square

Coaster Holder: 6⅜ inches W x 6⅛ inches H x 3 inches D

YOU'LL NEED

- ☐ 1 sheet regular 7-count plastic canvas
- ☐ 1 sheet Darice Ultra Stiff 7-count plastic canvas
- ☐ Worsted weight yarn as listed in color key
- ☐ Kreinik Heavy (#32) Braid as listed in color key
- ☐ DMC #5 pearl cotton as listed in color key
- ☐ #16 tapestry needle
- ☐ Sheet off-white felt (optional)
- ☐ Tacky craft glue (optional)
- ☐ Low-temperature glue gun

INSTRUCTIONS

1 Cut coasters, crows, dogs and dog ears from regular plastic canvas; cut holder pieces from stiff plastic canvas according to graphs.

2 Following graphs throughout, stitch and Overcast crows, dogs and dog ears.

3 Stitch remaining pieces, working uncoded areas on coasters with off-white Continental Stitches. Work two coasters with sage green cars as graphed and two with light brown cars. Do not stitch uncoded area in center of base.

4 When background stitching is completed, work light yellow Straight Stitches on crows and a silver braid Straight Stitch for door handle on cars. Using 2 plies black yarn, stitch steering wheel, but do not use yarn to stitch steering column.

5 Using black pearl cotton throughout, work Backstitches and Straight Stitches on cars, dogs and steering column. Work French Knots for eyes on dogs.

6 Overcast coasters with off-white. If desired, cut felt to fit backs of coasters. Glue in place with tacky craft glue.

7 Overcast base and leaves on trees with kelly green. Whipstitch holder front and back to holder sides with dark brown and tan following graphs. Using kelly green, Whipstitch bottom edges of front, back and sides to base where indicated with blue line. Overcast remaining edges following graphs.

8 Using photo as a guide, with low-temperature glue gun, attach one ear to each dog, then glue one dog each to front and back along base. Glue one crow to each tree. ∎

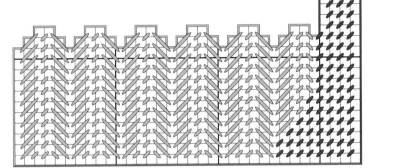

Classic Car Holder Front & Back
42 holes x 39 holes
Cut 2 from stiff

Classic Car Holder Side
11 holes x 13 holes
Cut 2 from stiff

Dog Ear
1 hole x 3 holes
Cut 2, from regular

Crow
4 holes x 4 holes
Cut 2, from regular

Dog
8 holes x 7 holes
Cut 2 from regular

COLOR KEY	
Plastic Canvas Yarn	**Yards**
☐ Tan	13
■ Kelly green	13
▨ Sage green	7
Light brown	7
■ Dark brown	4
▨ Medium brown	2
▨ Gray	2
■ Black	2
▨ Burgundy	1
☐ Yellow	1
■ Red	1
Uncoded areas on coasters are off-white Continental Stitches	
⁄ Off-white Overcasting	24
⁄ Light yellow Straight Stitch	
✗ Black Backstitch and Straight Stitch	1
Heavy (#32) Braid	
▨ Silver #001	
⁄ Silver #001 Straight Stitch	2
#5 Pearl Cotton	
⁄ Black #310 Backstitch and Straight Stitch	4
● Black #310 French Knot	
Color numbers given are for Kreinik Heavy (#32) Braid and DMC #5 pearl cotton	

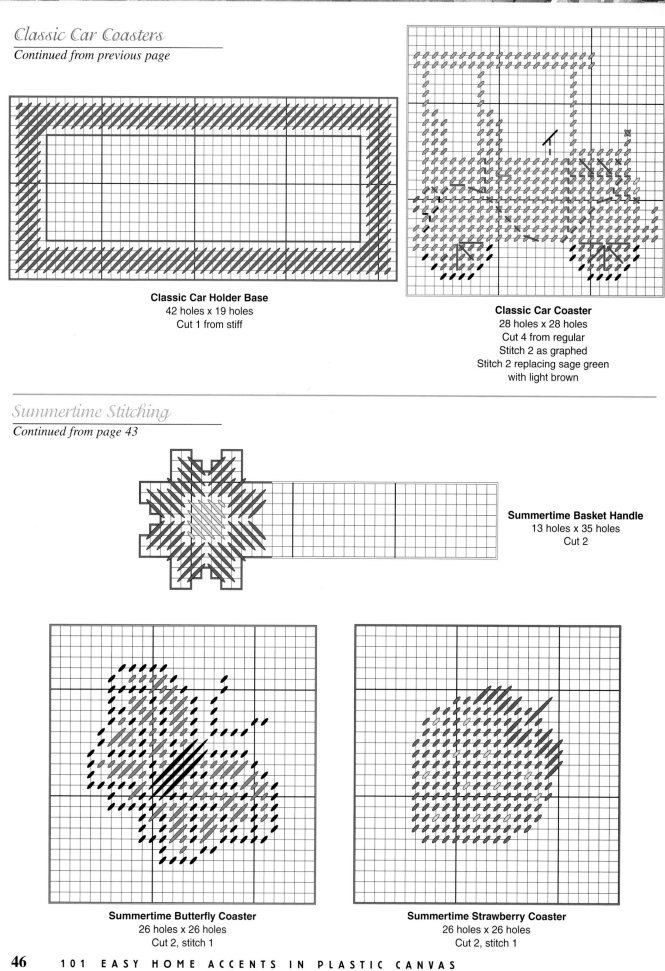

Classic Car Coasters
Continued from previous page

Classic Car Holder Base
42 holes x 19 holes
Cut 1 from stiff

Classic Car Coaster
28 holes x 28 holes
Cut 4 from regular
Stitch 2 as graphed
Stitch 2 replacing sage green
with light brown

Summertime Stitching
Continued from page 43

Summertime Basket Handle
13 holes x 35 holes
Cut 2

Summertime Butterfly Coaster
26 holes x 26 holes
Cut 2, stitch 1

Summertime Strawberry Coaster
26 holes x 26 holes
Cut 2, stitch 1

Anchor's Aweigh

*A sparkling gold anchor stands out against
a rich blue or red background on this set of nautical coasters!*

Design by Joan Green

TAKE NOTE

Skill Level: Beginner

Finished Size: 3⅞ inches square

YOU'LL NEED

- ☐ ⅔ sheet 7-count plastic canvas
- ☐ Spinrite Bernat Berella "4" worsted weight yarn as listed in color key
- ☐ ⅛-inch-wide Plastic Canvas 7 Metallic Needlepoint Yarn by Rainbow Gallery as listed in color key
- ☐ 1⁄16-inch-wide Plastic Canvas 10 Metallic Needlepoint Yarn by Rainbow Gallery as listed in color key
- ☐ #16 tapestry needle
- ☐ 8 inch x 8 inch piece royal blue self-adhesive Presto felt from Kunin Felt
- ☐ 8-inch x 8-inch piece red self-adhesive Presto felt from Kunin Felt

PROJECT NOTE

For better coverage, when stitching with navy worsted weight yarn, separate into two 2-ply strands, then put them back together for stitching.

INSTRUCTIONS

1 Cut plastic canvas according to graph.

2 Stitch coasters following graph and Project Note, working two coasters with navy as graphed and two replacing navy with scarlet. Overcast following graphs.

3 When background stitching and Overcasting are completed, work Backstitches and French Knots with 1⁄16-inch-wide gold metallic yarn.

4 Cut pieces of felt to fit coaster backs; attach royal blue felt to back of navy coasters and red felt to back of scarlet coasters. ◼

COLOR KEY	
Worsted Weight Yarn	**Yards**
◼ Scarlet #8933	16
◼ Navy #8965	16
⅛-Inch Metallic Needlepoint Yarn	
☐ Gold #PC1	3
1⁄16-Inch Metallic Needlepoint Yarn	
╱ Gold #PM51 Backstitch and Straight Stitch	½
● Gold #PM51 French Knot	
Color numbers given are for Spinrite Bernat Berella "4" worsted weight yarn and Rainbow Gallery ⅛-inch-wide Plastic Canvas 7 Metallic Needlepoint Yarn and 1⁄16-inch-wide Plastic Canvas 10 Metallic Needlepoint Yarn.	

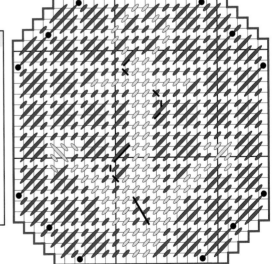

Anchor's Away Coaster
25 holes x 25 holes
Cut 4
Stitch 2 as graphed
Stitch 2 replacing navy with scarlet

Quilt Block Stars

Four different quilt star patterns worked in a rainbow of colors against a black background make this coaster set unique!

Design by Alida Macor

TAKE NOTE

Skill Level: Beginner

Finished Size:

Coasters: 4⅛ inches W x 4⅛ inches L

Coaster Holder: 4⅜ inches W x 2¼ inches H x 2¼ inches D

YOU'LL NEED

- ☐ 2 sheets clear 7-count plastic canvas
- ☐ ½ sheet black 7-count plastic canvas
- ☐ Uniek Needloft plastic canvas yarn as listed in color key
- ☐ Worsted weight yarn as listed in color key
- ☐ 2 sheets black self-adhesive Presto felt from Kunin Felt

INSTRUCTIONS

1 Cut eight coasters from clear plastic canvas and one holder front from black plastic canvas according to graphs.

2 From black plastic canvas, cut two 14-hole x 14-hole pieces for holder sides and two 28-hole x 14-hole pieces for holder back and holder bottom. All holder pieces will remain unstitched.

3 Stitch two coasters with each design following graphs. Overcast with baby yellow.

4 Cut eight 4-inch squares from felt and adhere to coaster backs.

5 Using black throughout, Whipstitch holder front and back to holder sides, then Whipstitch front, back and sides to holder bottom. Overcast all remaining edges. ■

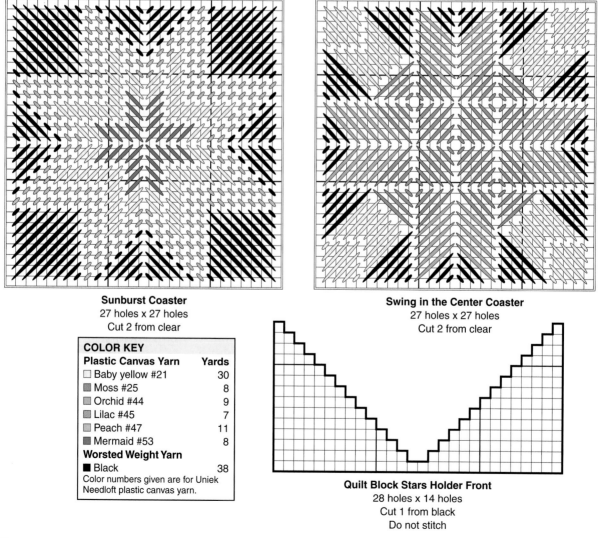

Sunburst Coaster
27 holes x 27 holes
Cut 2 from clear

Swing in the Center Coaster
27 holes x 27 holes
Cut 2 from clear

COLOR KEY	
Plastic Canvas Yarn	**Yards**
☐ Baby yellow #21	30
▨ Moss #25	8
▨ Orchid #44	9
▨ Lilac #45	7
▨ Peach #47	11
▨ Mermaid #53	8
Worsted Weight Yarn	
■ Black	38
Color numbers given are for Uniek Needloft plastic canvas yarn.	

Quilt Block Stars Holder Front
28 holes x 14 holes
Cut 1 from black
Do not stitch

God's Eye Coaster
27 holes x 27 holes
Cut 2 from clear

Indian Patch Coaster
27 holes x 27 holes
Cut 2 from clear

Japanese Kimonos

Bring a touch of the Orient into your home with this detailed and colorful set of kimono coasters!

Design by Celia Lange Designs

TAKE NOTE

Skill Level: Beginner

Finished Size:

Coasters: 3¼ inches W x 3½ inches L

Coaster Holder: 4½ inches W x 4⅜ inches H x 3 inches D

YOU'LL NEED

- ☐ 2 sheets Darice Ultra Stiff 7-count plastic canvas
- ☐ Coats & Clark Red Heart Super Saver worsted weight yarn Art. E301 as listed in color key
- ☐ ⅛-inch-wide Plastic Canvas 7 Metallic Needlepoint Yarn by Rainbow Gallery as listed in color key
- ☐ 1/16-inch-wide Plastic Canvas 10 Metallic Needlepoint Yarn by Rainbow Gallery as listed in color key
- ☐ DMC #3 pearl cotton as listed in color key
- ☐ #16 tapestry needle
- ☐ 1 sheet white Fun Foam craft foam by Westrim Crafts
- ☐ Hot-glue gun

INSTRUCTIONS

1 Cut plastic canvas according to graphs (this page and page 52). Cut one 29-hole x 19-hole piece for holder base, one 29-hole x 19-hole piece for lid bottom, one 25-hole x 15-hole piece for box bottom and one 23-hole x 13-hole piece for inner lid.

2 Work holder base, box bottom, lid bottom and inner lid with black yarn Continental Stitches. Stitch remaining pieces following graphs, working kimono on one coaster A with raspberry as graphed, and one with teal. Work kimono on one coaster B with purple as graphed and one with royal.

3 When background stitching is completed, work raspberry, royal, teal and purple yarn Backstitches on corresponding kimonos on coasters, and 1/16-inch-wide gold metallic needlepoint yarn Backstitches on frames and coasters.

4 Using pearl cotton throughout, work black Backstitches on screens and on raspberry and teal kimonos; work medium nile green Backstitches on purple and royal kimonos. Work white French Knots on raspberry and purple kimonos and light mauve French Knots on teal and royal kimonos.

5 Overcast coasters with soft white. Cut craft foam slightly smaller than coasters and glue to backsides.

6 Using black yarn through step 7, Overcast side screens, holder base, all lid pieces and top and inside edges of frames. Cut craft foam slightly smaller than side screens, then glue to backsides.

7 To form coaster box, Whipstitch wrong sides of back screens together, then glue to backside of frame back. Center and glue right side of one side screen to backside of each frame side. Whipstitch frame sides to frame back, then Whipstitch sides to frame front. Whipstitch front, back and sides to box bottom.

8 Center and glue box to holder base. Glue wrong sides of lid top and lid bottom together. Center and glue wrong side of inner lid to lid bottom.

9 Slide one coaster into box directly behind frame front for display. Place remaining coasters behind display coaster. ∎

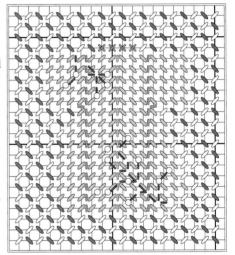

Japanese Kimono Coaster A
21 holes x 23 holes
Cut 2
Stitch 1 as graphed
Stitch 1 with teal kimono
and light mauve French Knots

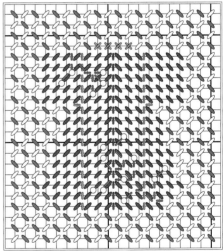

Japanese Kimono Coaster B
21 holes x 23 holes
Cut 2
Stitch 1 as graphed
Stitch 1 with royal kimono
and light mauve French Knots

Japanese Kimonos
Continued from previous page

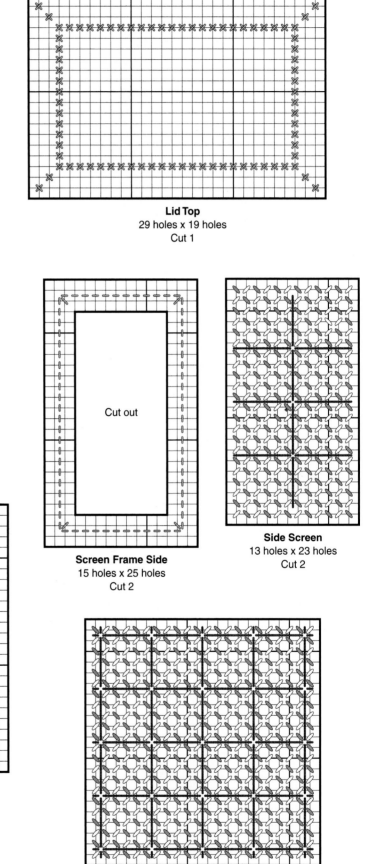

Lid Top
29 holes x 19 holes
Cut 1

COLOR KEY

Worsted Weight Yarn	Yards
■ Aran #313	30
□ Soft white #316	16
■ Purple #357	4
☐ Raspberry #375	4
Royal #385	4
Teal #388	4
Uncoded areas are black #312 Continental Stitches	71
✦ Black #312 Overcasting and Whipstitching	
✦ Purple #357 Backstitch	
✦ Raspberry #375 Backstitch	
¹/₈-Inch Metallic Needlepoint Yarn	**5**
☐ Gold #PC1	
¹/₁₆-Inch Metallic Needlepoint Yarn	
✦ Gold #PM51 Backstitch	
#3 Pearl Cotton	**6**
✦ Black #310 Backstitch	2
✦ Medium nile green #913 Backstitch	2
○ White French Knot	2
Light mauve #3689 French Knot	

Color numbers given are for Coats & Clark Red Heart Super Saver worsted weight yarn Art. E301, Rainbow Gallery ¹/₈-inch-wide Plastic Canvas 7 Metallic Needlepoint Yarn and ¹/₁₆-inch-wide Plastic Canvas 10 Metallic Needlepoint Yarn and DMC #3 Pearl Cotton.

Screen Frame Side
15 holes x 25 holes
Cut 2

Side Screen
13 holes x 23 holes
Cut 2

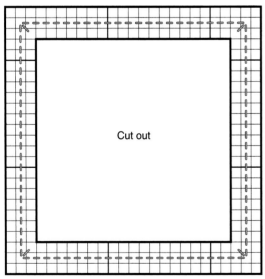

Screen Frame Front & Back
25 holes x 25 holes
Cut 2

Back Screen
23 holes x 23 holes
Cut 2

Delightful Door Decor

*Share your love of stitching with every visitor to your home
by creating an ever-changing collection of door decorations
to suit the season of year and your own unique style!*

Sand, Surf & Sails

If you listen carefully, you'll almost be able to hear the waves crashing and seagulls calling as you stitch this handsome decoration.

Design by Celia Lange Designs

TAKE NOTE

Skill Level: Intermediate

Finished Size: 12 inches W x 13¾ inches H

YOU'LL NEED

☐ 2 sheets Darice Ultra Stiff 7-count plastic canvas

☐ Small amount black 7-count plastic canvas

☐ Coats & Clark Red Heart Classic worsted weight yarn Art. E267 as listed in color key

☐ Coats & Clark Red Heart Super Saver worsted weight yarn Art. E301 as listed in color key

☐ #16 tapestry needle

☐ Nylon fishing line

☐ Hot-glue gun

INSTRUCTIONS

1 Cut seagulls from black plastic canvas according to graphs, cutting away blue lines around legs and beaks. Cut beaks to a point.

2 Cut remaining pieces from stiff plastic canvas according to graphs.

3 Overcast standing seagull following graph. Stitch remaining pieces following graphs, working uncoded areas with white Continental Stitches and reversing one flying seagull before stitching.

4 Overcast pieces following graphs.

5 When stitching and Overcasting are completed, work Straight Stitches on lighthouse with 4 plies black and French Knots on seagulls with 2 plies black.

ASSEMBLY

1 Use photo as a guide throughout assembly.

2 Glue sails to backside of boat, sun center to sun, and standing seagull to sand on beach.

3 Glue lighthouse and assembled sailboat to backside of beach, then glue to bottom of sky archway. Center and glue sun to top of archway, then center and glue cloud to archway below sun.

4 Thread and secure one end of nylon fishing line down through backside of cloud where indicated at arrow. Thread line through backside of one left-facing flying seagull at wing and head, then down through backside of beach.

5 Thread through backside of beach, coming back up approximately ¾ inch from first line. Thread through backside of right-facing flying seagull at wing/tail and then through wing/tail of first seagull.

6 Continue threading fishing line through cloud, seagulls and beach until all three seagulls are strung as in photo. Tie off fishing line securely. Slide seagulls up and down to position as desired. ■

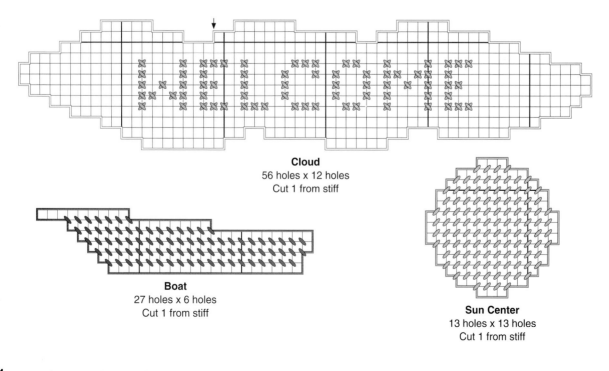

Cloud
56 holes x 12 holes
Cut 1 from stiff

Boat
27 holes x 6 holes
Cut 1 from stiff

Sun Center
13 holes x 13 holes
Cut 1 from stiff

Lighthouse
17 holes x 36 holes
Cut 1 from stiff

Standing Seagull
6 holes x 4 holes
Cut 1 from black
Cut away blue lines

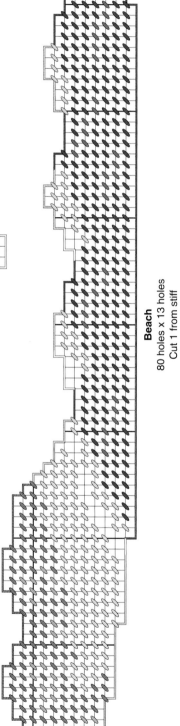

Beach
80 holes x 13 holes
Cut 1 from stiff

COLOR KEY

Worsted Weight Yarn	Yards
☐ White #1	2
■ Black #12	10
☐ Cornmeal #220	1
☐ Yellow #230	1
☐ Maize #261	6
☐ Gold #321	2
☐ Buff #334	4
■ Coffee #365	4
■ Nickel #401	1
☐ Silver #412	2
■ Peacock green #508	26
☐ Blue jewel	7
■ True blue	1
■ Light periwinkle	5
■ Cherry red	
Uncoded areas are white	17
#1 Continental Stitches	
✏ Black Straight Stitch	
● Black French Knot	

Color numbers given are for Coats & Clark
Red Heart Classic worsted weight yarn Art.
E267 and Super Saver worsted weight yarn
Art. E301.

Flying Seagull
9 holes x 3 holes
Cut 3, reverse 1, from black
Cut away blue lines

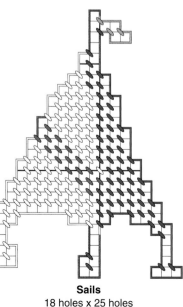

Sails
18 holes x 25 holes
Cut 1 from stiff

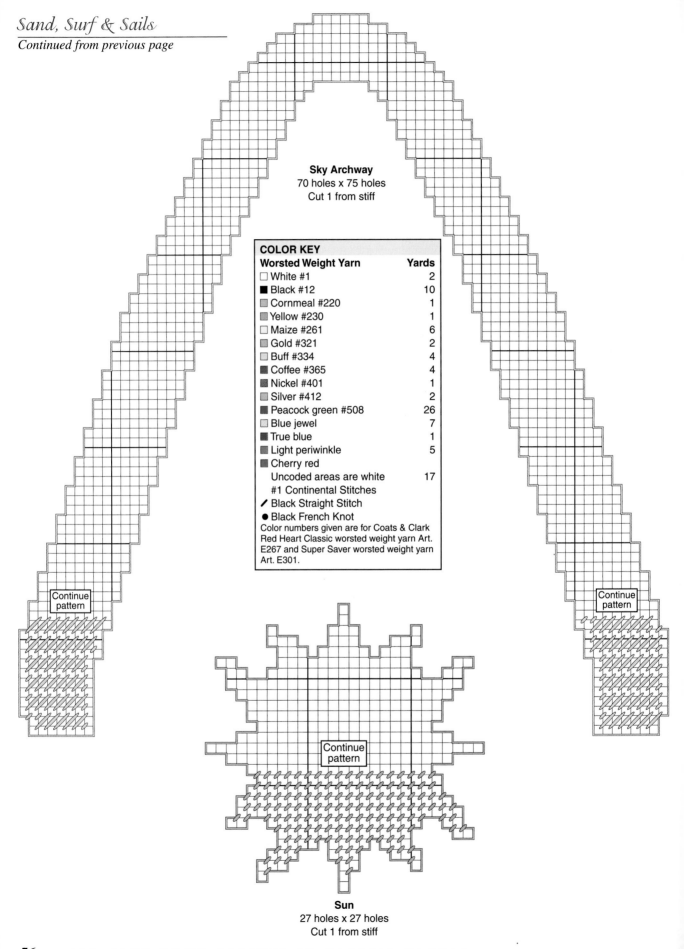

Sky Archway
70 holes x 75 holes
Cut 1 from stiff

COLOR KEY

Worsted Weight Yarn	Yards
☐ White #1	2
◼ Black #12	10
▨ Cornmeal #220	1
▨ Yellow #230	1
☐ Maize #261	6
▨ Gold #321	2
☐ Buff #334	4
◼ Coffee #365	4
▨ Nickel #401	1
▨ Silver #412	2
◼ Peacock green #508	26
☐ Blue jewel	7
◼ True blue	1
▨ Light periwinkle	5
◼ Cherry red	
Uncoded areas are white	17
#1 Continental Stitches	
╱ Black Straight Stitch	
● Black French Knot	

Color numbers given are for Coats & Clark
Red Heart Classic worsted weight yarn Art.
E267 and Super Saver worsted weight yarn
Art. E301.

Continue pattern

Continue pattern

Continue pattern

Sun
27 holes x 27 holes
Cut 1 from stiff

Fresh Eggs Doorstop

*Country lovers will enjoy using this clever doorstop to prop open
the kitchen door while bustling in and out to set the dining room table!*

Design by Celia Lange Designs

TAKE NOTE

Skill Level: Beginner

Finished Size: 7 inches W x 8¼ inches
H x 3⅞ inches D

YOU'LL NEED

- ☐ 1 sheet Darice Ultra Stiff 7-count
  plastic canvas
- ☐ Coats & Clark Red Heart Classic
  worsted weight yarn Art. E267 as
  listed in color key
- ☐ DMC 6-strand embroidery floss as
  listed in color key

- ☐ Coats & Clark Red Heart Super
  Saver worsted weight yarn Art. E301
  as listed in color key
- ☐ #16 tapestry needle
- ☐ Yellow plastic-covered wire coat
  hanger
- ☐ Wire cutters
- ☐ 2 (2-inch x 1-inch) strips blue Fun
  Foam craft foam by Westrim Craft
- ☐ Block floral clay
- ☐ Plastic wrap
- ☐ Tan or brown paper shred

- ☐ White and brown plastic eggs
- ☐ Hot-glue gun

INSTRUCTIONS

1 Cut plastic canvas according to
graphs (page 58).

2 Stitch pieces following graphs,
working uncoded areas on hen
pieces with bronze Continental Stitches.
Stitch center area on basket back entirely with skipper blue Continental
Stitches, eliminating the words "FRESH
EGGS."

3 Work black floss French Knot on hen when background stitching is completed. Overcast nest and hen pieces following graphs.

4 Using photo as a guide throughout assembly and using skipper blue through step 5, Overcast top edges of basket front, back and sides. Whipstitch front and back to sides, then Whipstitch front, back and sides to bottom.

5 For basket handle, cut a 16-inch length of coat hanger with wire cutters. Bend hanger to fit inside basket from side to side. Overcast side edges of plastic canvas basket handles. Place coat hanger between pieces and Whipstitch together along remaining edges.

6 Glue wire handle inside basket to basket sides, then secure by gluing strips of fun foam over wire ends.

7 Glue nest and wing to hen, then glue hen to right side of basket front, making sure bottom edges are even.

8 Shape floral clay into a block to fit in bottom of basket; wrap with plastic wrap. Glue block to inside bottom for weight. Fill basket with paper shred and plastic eggs. ■

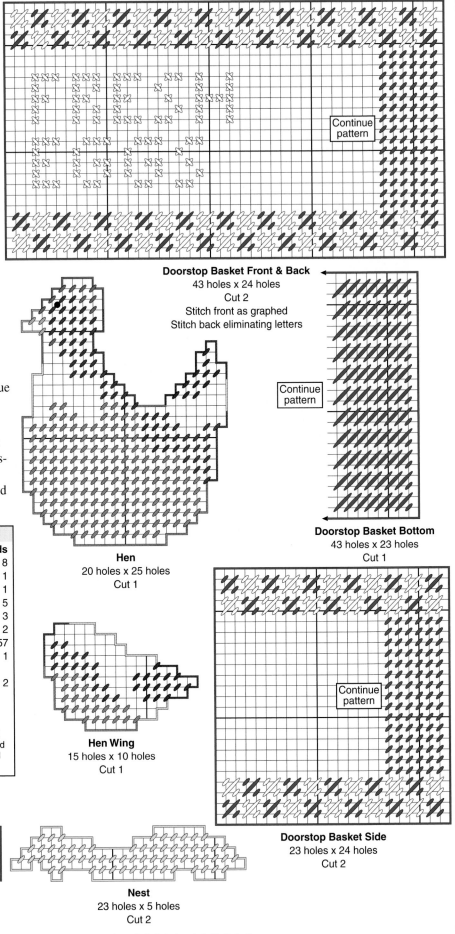

Doorstop Basket Front & Back
43 holes x 24 holes
Cut 2
Stitch front as graphed
Stitch back eliminating letters

Doorstop Basket Bottom
43 holes x 23 holes
Cut 1

Hen
20 holes x 25 holes
Cut 1

Hen Wing
15 holes x 10 holes
Cut 1

Doorstop Basket Side
23 holes x 24 holes
Cut 2

Doorstop Basket Handle
19 holes x 5 holes
Cut 2

Nest
23 holes x 5 holes
Cut 2

COLOR KEY

Worsted Weight Yarn	Yards
☐ Off-white #03	8
▨ Gold #321	1
■ Brown #328	1
▨ Warm brown #336	5
▨ Mid brown #339	3
☐ Honey gold #645	2
■ Skipper blue #848	57
■ Country red #914	1
Uncoded areas on hen pieces are bronze #286 Continental Stitches	2
∕ Bronze #286 Overcasting	

6-Strand Embroidery Floss
● Black #310 French Knot

Color numbers given are for Coats & Clark Red Heart Classic worsted weight yarn Art. E267 and Super Saver worsted weight yarn Art. E301 and DMC 6-strand embroidery floss.

Garden Entrance

Hung on your back door or garden gate, this charming sign
will give a warm welcome to all flower-lovers.

Design by Janelle Giese

Silly Scarecrows Wreath

These silly scarecrows are dancing an autumn jig!
Stitch them along with their crow companions, for a country touch!

Design by Judy Collishaw

TAKE NOTE

Skill Level: Beginner

Finished Size: 16¼ inches W x 25¼ inches H with bow

YOU'LL NEED

- ☐ 1 artist-size sheet 7-count plastic canvas
- ☐ Worsted weight yarn as listed in color key
- ☐ DMC #5 pearl cotton as listed in color key
- ☐ #16 tapestry needle
- ☐ 14-inch natural willow wreath
- ☐ 6 yards natural raffia
- ☐ 8½ yards ⅝-inch-wide terra-cotta ribbon
- ☐ 4 inches florist wire
- ☐ Low-temperature glue gun

INSTRUCTIONS

1. Cut plastic canvas according to graphs.

2. Stitch and Overcast pieces following graphs, reversing two crows before stitching. On scarecrows, work French Knot and Backstitched eyes with 2 plies black yarn. Backstitch mouths with Christmas red pearl cotton.

3. Using photo as a guide through step 7, cut one yard each of ribbon and raffia. Wrap ribbon around wreath, then raffia, gluing ends in place at bottom of wreath.

4. Make a multi-looped bow with 7 yards ribbon. Twist florist wire around center of bow to hold loops in place. Cut remaining ribbon in half; glue halves to bottom front of wreath for streamers. Glue bow over top of streamers.

5. Make three smaller bows with remaining raffia, allowing one bow to have 12-inch long streamers. Glue bow with streamers to center front of ribbon bow and remaining raffia bows at each side of ribbon bow.

6. Tie a 3-inch loop in ½ yard raffia, then tie raffia around top of wreath for hanger. Trim ends.

7. Glue center scarecrow to top center front of wreath. Glue left scarecrow to front left side and right scarecrow to front right side. Glue two crows to each side of wreath front. ▪

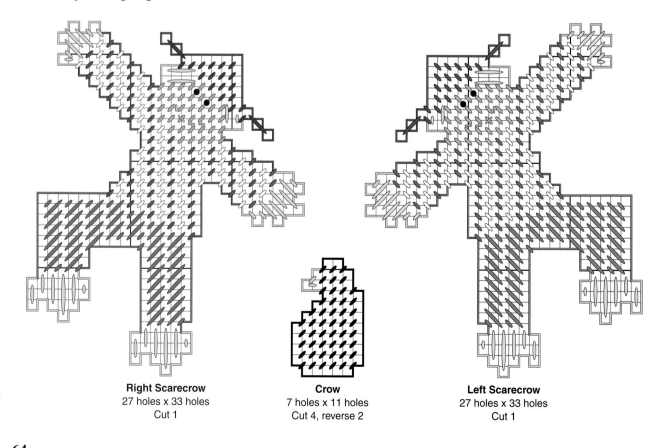

Right Scarecrow
27 holes x 33 holes
Cut 1

Crow
7 holes x 11 holes
Cut 4, reverse 2

Left Scarecrow
27 holes x 33 holes
Cut 1

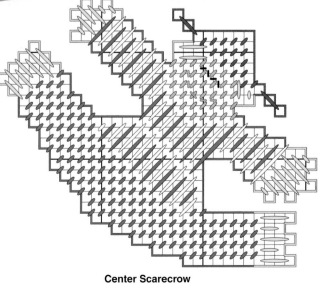

COLOR KEY

Worsted Weight Yarn	Yards
■ Country blue	7
■ Red	6
■ Black	5
□ Off-white	4
▫ Mustard	4
■ Curry	3
▫ Light tan	2
✎ Black Backstitch	
● Black French Knot	

#5 Pearl Cotton

✎ Christmas red #321 Backstitch	1

Color number given is for DMC #5 pearl cotton.

Center Scarecrow
31 holes x 25 holes
Cut 1

Friendly Froggy Door Hanger

If your child or grandchild loves frogs, he or she is sure to be delighted with this whimsical project!

Design by Joyce Keklock

TAKE NOTE

Skill Level: Beginner

Finished Size: 6 inches W x 13¼ inches H

YOU'LL NEED

- ½ sheet 7-count plastic canvas
- Uniek Needloft plastic canvas yarn as listed in color key
- #16 tapestry needle
- 4 green chenille stems
- 2 (12mm) movable eyes
- Hot-glue gun

INSTRUCTIONS

1 Cut plastic canvas according to graphs (page 68).

2 Stitch pieces following graphs. When background stitching is completed, work Christmas red Backstitches for mouth on head.

3 Overcast head, hands and feet with holly. For body, Overcast top edge with fern and all remaining inside and outside edges with holly.

4 For one arm, cut one 8-inch length of chenille stem and insert ½ inch through one upper hole in body; twist to secure. Cut nine 24-inch lengths of holly yarn. Pull all lengths through same upper hole to middle of lengths and fold, covering chenille stem and making sure ends are even.

5 Divide yarn into three groups of six strands. Holding chenille stem with center group of yarn, braid until ½ inch of chenille stem is left. With chenille stem at back of braid, tie securely with another length of holly yarn. Trim so ends are even.

6 Repeat steps 3 and 4 for remaining arm and two legs.

7 Using photo as a guide through step 7, glue ends of arms to side edges of hands. Glue ends of legs to center top edge of feet.

8 Glue head to body and movable eyes to head. Bend arms and legs into desired position. ∎

COLOR KEY	
Plastic Canvas Yarn	**Yards**
☐ Fern #23	2
■ Holly #27	32
✎ Christmas red #02 Backstitch	1
Color numbers given are for Uniek Needloft plastic canvas yarn.	

Graphs continued on page 68

Textured Doorstop

Prop open the door to the den with this handsome and richly-colored doorstop!

Design by Celia Lange Designs

TAKE NOTE

Skill Level: Beginner

Finished Size: 7⅞ inches W x 4¼ inches H x 2¾ inches D

YOU'LL NEED

- ☐ 2 sheets Darice Ultra Stiff 7-count plastic canvas
- ☐ Coats & Clark Red Heart Classic worsted weight yarn Art. E267 as listed in color key
- ☐ #16 tapestry needle
- ☐ Brick

INSTRUCTIONS

1 Cut plastic canvas according to graphs (this page and page 68).

2 Stitch pieces following graphs, working purple and red sections first, then blue sections. Work purple Backstitches in a zigzag pattern over blue stitches.

3 Using Olympic blue throughout, Whipstitch front and back to sides, then Whipstitch front, back and sides to bottom. Place brick in doorstop; Whipstitch top to front, back and sides. ▪

COLOR KEY	
Worsted Weight Yarn	**Yards**
▨ Amethyst #588	11
▪ Purple #596	15
▨ New berry #760	14
▨ Skipper blue #848	18
▪ Olympic blue #849	18
▨ Cardinal #760	14
╱ Purple #596 Backstitch	

Color numbers given are for Coats & Clark Red Heart Classic worsted weight yarn Art. E267.

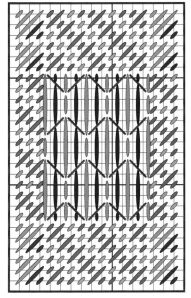

Doorstop Side
17 holes x 27 holes
Cut 2

Textured Doorstop
Continued from previous page

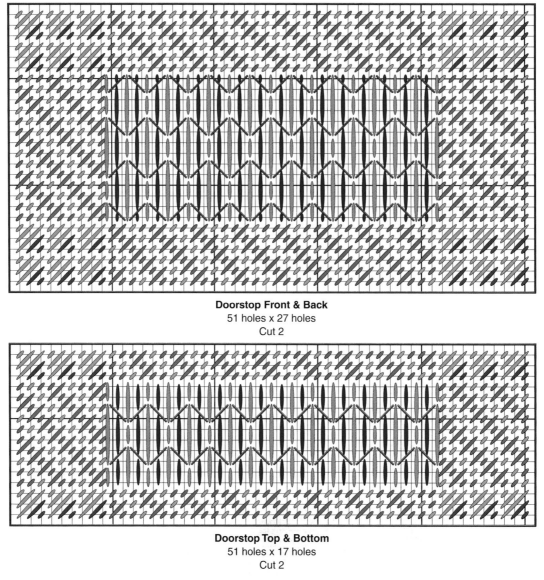

Doorstop Front & Back
51 holes x 27 holes
Cut 2

Doorstop Top & Bottom
51 holes x 17 holes
Cut 2

Friendly Froggy Door Hanger
Continued from page 66

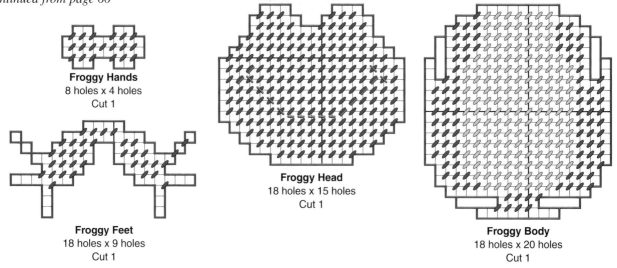

Froggy Hands
8 holes x 4 holes
Cut 1

Froggy Feet
18 holes x 9 holes
Cut 1

Froggy Head
18 holes x 15 holes
Cut 1

Froggy Body
18 holes x 20 holes
Cut 1

Star-Spangled Welcome

*Red, white and blue stars and jingling golden bells make
this welcome sign an all-American favorite!*

Design by Ruby Thacker

TAKE NOTE

Skill Level: Intermediate

Finished Size: Approximately
10½ inches W x 14¼ inches H,
excluding hanger

YOU'LL NEED

- ☐ 1 sheet Darice Ultra Stiff 7-count plastic canvas
- ☐ Uniek Needloft plastic canvas yarn as listed in color key
- ☐ #16 tapestry needle
- ☐ 3 yards gold lamé thread
- ☐ 4 (25mm) gold liberty bells

INSTRUCTIONS

1 Cut plastic canvas according to graphs.

2 Stitch pieces following graphs, working uncoded area on banner with dark royal Continental Stitches. Stitch one large star with red as graphed, two with white and two with dark royal. Overcast all pieces with adjacent colors.

3 Using photo as a guide, overlap and glue large stars in a slight arch following top edge of banner and placing red star in center, white stars under red on each side and one blue star under each white star.

4 Using a double strand gold lamé thread through step 5, attach large red star to top of banner where indicated where indicated on graphs, allowing ¼ inch between star and top of banner.

5 Attach small star to center bottom of banner where indicated on graphs, allowing 1½ inches between. Attach remaining bells to bottom of banner where indicated, allowing 1 inch between banner and inner bells and 2¼ inches between banner and outer bells.

6 For hanger, cut two 12-inch lengths of gold lamé thread; place lengths together. Thread ends through top holes of white stars; knot and trim ends. ■

COLOR KEY

Worsted Weight Yarn	Yards
■ Red	9
☐ White	14
Uncoded areas are dark royal #48 Continental Stitches	24
■ Dark royal #46 Overcasting	
○ Attach star to banner	
● Attach bell	

Color numbers given are for Uniek Needloft plastic canvas yarn.

Small Star
17 holes x 16 holes
Cut 1

Large Star
21 holes x 21 holes
Cut 5
Stitch 1 as graphed
Stitch 2 with white
Stitch 2 with dark royal

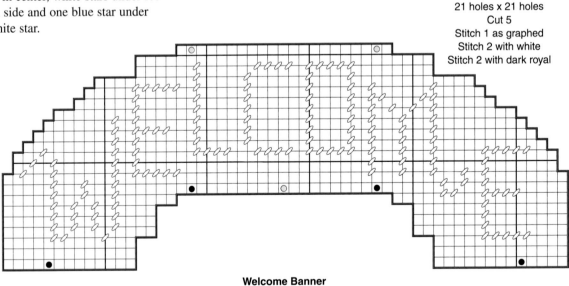

Welcome Banner
55 holes x 21 holes
Cut 1

Welcome Friends

*Greet friends and family with this country-warm welcome sign.
It looks great over a door or fireplace mantel!*

Design by Darla J. Fanton

TAKE NOTE

Skill Level: Intermediate

Finished Size: 31¼ inches W x
3⅞ inches H

YOU'LL NEED

- 2½ artist-size sheets Darice Ultra Stiff 7-count plastic canvas
- Worsted weight yarn as listed in color key
- #16 tapestry needle
- 2 sawtooth hangers

INSTRUCTIONS

1 Cut plastic canvas according to graphs (page 72). Cut one 25 hole x 69 hole piece and two 25 hole x 68 hole pieces for middle layer. Cut two 25 hole x 103 hole pieces for backing. Backing will remain unstitched.

2 Place middle layer pieces behind top pieces and stitch as one, following graphs. *Note: There will be a one-hole space between right and left halves of top layer and a one-hole space between*

pieces of middle layer. Work uncoded background with off-white Continental Stitches. Straight Stitch heart with a double strand of dark rose.

3 Place backing pieces on wrong side of stitched sign; Whipstitch together through all layers with medium brown, stitching twice in each hole to cover.

4 Attach sawtooth hangers to back as desired. ∎

Graphs continued on page 72

Welcome Friends

Continued from previous page

COLOR KEY	
Plastic Canvas Yarn	**Yards**
■ Medium brown	35
■ Sage green	14
■ Dark rose	2
Uncoded areas are off-white	
Continental Stitches	48

Tips & Techniques

I am always looking for new ways to recycle. The following hint is an excellent way to recycle prescription containers and 2-pound Velveeta cheese boxes.

Keep your pins and needles neat and organized by storing them in the clear, flat prescription containers. Use the small, round containers for small items such as beads, sequins, spangles, jewels, wiggle eyes, etc. used on crafts. Label each one on the top.

Sit round containers in the Velveeta box for each access. The box will hold 10 small containers or four larger ones plus two square flat boxes.

—A. Marie Connor, Illinois

Empty cardboard craft ribbon spools make very good spools for ribbon you purchase by the yard. Scotch tape starting end of ribbon to cardboard spool. Wrap ribbon around until you come to the end, then tape this end to the outside of the spool.

For ribbons larger than ¼-inch, use the cardboard roll from paper towels or toilet tissue.

—A. Marie Connor, Illinois

A wire coat hanger makes a handy rack for spools of craft ribbon. By untwisting the top part of the hanger and slipping spools over the end, ribbons are ready to use.

After placing ribbon spools on wire, twist top back together. Hang close to work area. There is no need to take spools off hanger—just unwind ribbon and snip off what you need. Then remember to Scotch tape cut end of ribbon back to spool.

—A. Marie Connor, Illinois

Sign Right Half
103 holes x 25 holes
Cut 1

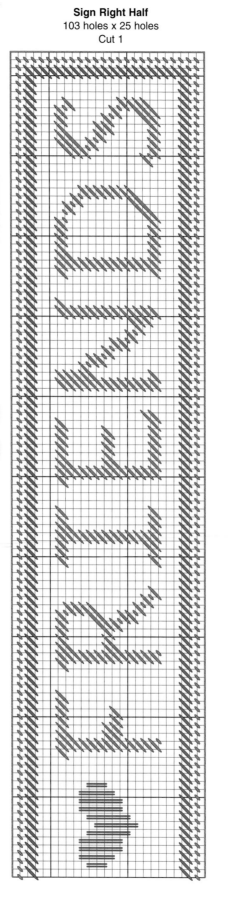

Sign Left Half
103 holes x 25 holes
Cut 1

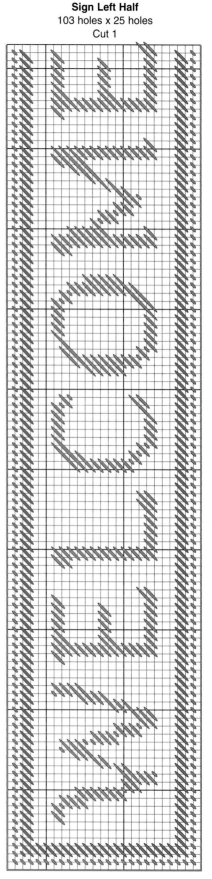

Outdoor Accents

Whether your favorite outdoor spot is on the patio or in the garden, you'll love dressing it up with an assortment of tinkling wind chimes, flowerpot accents, garden signs and much more!

Tiered Birdhouse

*This charming birdhouse will make a sweet display in your flower garden.
Hang it from a wrought-iron plant holder to see it gently swing in the breeze!*

Design by Celia Lange Designs

TAKE NOTE

Skill Level: Intermediate

Finished Size: 4¼ inches W x 8⅜ inches H x 4 inches D, excluding hanger

YOU'LL NEED

- 2 sheets Darice Ultra Stiff 7-count plastic canvas
- Darice Nylon Plus plastic canvas yarn as listed in color key
- DMC #3 pearl cotton as listed in color key
- #16 tapestry needle
- 3 toothpicks
- Yellow acrylic paint
- Paintbrush
- Mushroom birds: 2 yellow and 1 pink
- Small amount Spanish moss
- Hot-glue gun

CUTTING & STITCHING

1 Cut plastic canvas according to graphs.

2 Stitch pieces following graphs, working uncoded areas with white Continental Stitches. Work only the two outer rows of teal blue on upper platform.

3 When background stitching is completed, work embroidery on front pieces with pearl cotton.

4 With teal, Overcast bottom edges of upper house pieces; Overcast top and bottom edges of lower house pieces. Overcast platform edges.

5 Overcast openings on fronts with yellow. Overcast top edges of upper front, back and sides with white.

ASSEMBLY

1 Using teal blue throughout, Whipstitch corresponding fronts, backs and sides together. Whipstitch top edges of roof pieces together; Overcast remaining roof edges.

2 For hanger, cut a 6-inch length of teal blue. Thread ends through holes indicated to wrong side of roof; knot on inside, making a 2½-inch loop.

3 Paint toothpicks with yellow acrylic paint. Allow to dry. Cut ¾ inches off each end; glue ends in holes indicated below each opening.

4 Using photo as a guide and centering pieces throughout assembly, glue lower house to bottom platform. Glue

scraps of Spanish moss in opening, then glue wrong side of upper platform to top edge of lower house.

5 Glue upper house to upper platform, then glue scraps of Spanish moss in both openings. Glue roof to upper house.

6 Glue one bird to each platform, then glue remaining bird to roof with a small amount of Spanish moss under it. ■

COLOR KEY

Plastic Canvas Yarn	Yards
■ Teal blue #08	41
■ Watermelon #54	13
■ Mermaid green #60	5
Uncoded areas are white #01 Continental Stitches	54
⁄ White #01 Overcasting	
⁄ Yellow #26 Overcasting	1
#3 Pearl Cotton	
⁄ Very dark gray green #924 Backstitch	1
ᕤ Dark rose #309 Lazy Daisy	1
○ Light topaz #726 French Knot	1
● Attach hanger	
● Attach toothpick perch	
Color numbers given are for Darice Nylon Plus plastic canvas yarn and DMC #3 pearl cotton.	

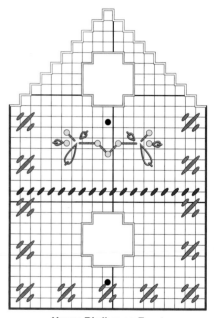

Upper Birdhouse Front
19 holes x 28 holes
Cut 1

Lower Birdhouse Back & Side
19 holes x 19 holes
Cut 3

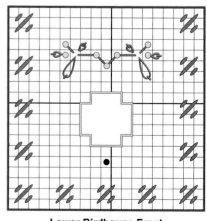

Lower Birdhouse Front
19 holes x 19 holes
Cut 1

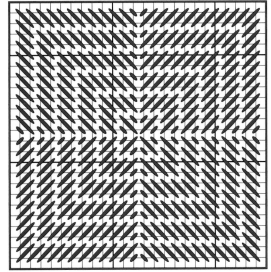

Lower Platform
25 holes x 25 holes
Cut 1
Stitch as graphed

Upper Platform
25 holes x 25 holes
Cut 1
Stitch outer two rows only

Birdhouse Roof
25 holes x 18 holes
Cut 2

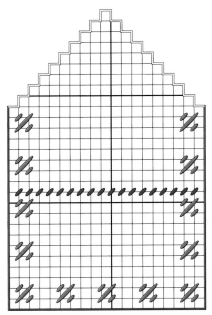

Upper Birdhouse Back
19 holes x 28 holes
Cut 1

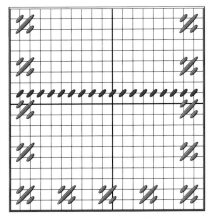

Upper Birdhouse Side
19 holes x 19 holes
Cut 2

I Love Gardening

Gardeners will love this pretty sign. Hang it on your patio door or garden gate!

Design by Celia Lange Designs

TAKE NOTE

Skill Level: Beginner

Finished Size: 8⅛ inches W x 10½ inches H

YOU'LL NEED

- ☐ 1 sheet Darice Ultra Stiff 7-count plastic canvas
- ☐ Coats & Clark Red Heart Classic worsted weight yarn Art. E267 as listed in color key
- ☐ DMC 6-strand embroidery floss as listed in color key
- ☐ #16 tapestry needle
- ☐ 7¾-inch x 1⅞-inch strip off-white Fun Foam craft foam by Westrim Crafts
- ☐ ¾-inch plastic or resin butterfly
- ☐ Small amount burgundy and off-white silk flowers
- ☐ Nylon fishing line
- ☐ Hot-glue gun

INSTRUCTIONS

1 Cut plastic canvas according to graphs.

2 Stitch pieces following graphs, working uncoded areas on sign and seed packet with eggshell Continental Stitches.

3 Overcast pieces following graphs, then embroider words on sign with yarn and words on seed packet with embroidery floss.

4 Using photo as a guide through step 8, glue sprinkler head and butterfly to watering can. Glue heart to sign between words.

5 Glue burgundy flowers to seed packet. Glue off-white flowers between flowerpot and pot rim.

6 Thread nylon fishing line through back of sign and flowerpot, allowing 1 to 1½ inches between pieces; tie ends in a secure knot. Repeat with watering can and seed packet.

7 For hanger, cut a 1 yard length of both country blue and medium coral rose yarn. Place lengths together and twist ends in opposite directions until it begins to loop back on itself. Place ends together, folding yarn in half; allow halves to twist around each other. Knot ends at desired length, then glue to back of sign.

8 Glue craft foam to back of sign. ∎

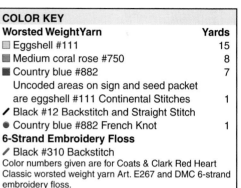

COLOR KEY

Worsted Weight Yarn	Yards
☐ Eggshell #111	15
▨ Medium coral rose #750	8
■ Country blue #882	7
Uncoded areas on sign and seed packet are eggshell #111 Continental Stitches	1
╱ Black #12 Backstitch and Straight Stitch	
● Country blue #882 French Knot	1
6-Strand Embroidery Floss	
╱ Black #310 Backstitch	

Color numbers given are for Coats & Clark Red Heart Classic worsted weight yarn Art. E267 and DMC 6-strand embroidery floss.

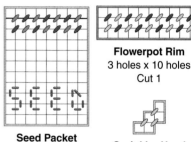

Flowerpot Rim
3 holes x 10 holes
Cut 1

Seed Packet
8 holes x 11 holes
Cut 1

Sprinkler Head
3 holes x 3 holes
Cut 1

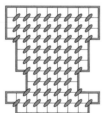

Flowerpot
9 holes x 10 holes
Cut 1

Heart
5 holes x 5 holes
Cut 1

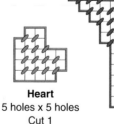

Watering Can
19 holes x 13 holes
Cut 1

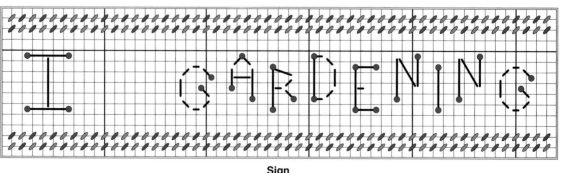

Sign
54 holes x 14 holes
Cut 1

Hummingbird Hut Wind Chime

Hummingbirds and flowers are a favorite summertime motif.
Stitch this colorful project and hang it from a tree or door to tinkle and chime!

Design by Janelle Giese

TAKE NOTE

Skill Level: Beginner

Finished Size: 5¾ inches W x 5 inches H, excluding hanger and wind chimes

YOU'LL NEED

- ☐ ½ sheet 7-count plastic canvas
- ☐ Small amount 10-count plastic canvas
- ☐ Uniek Needloft plastic canvas yarn as listed in color key
- ☐ DMC #3 pearl cotton as listed in color key
- ☐ DMC #5 pearl cotton as listed in color key
- ☐ DMC #8 pearl cotton as listed in color key
- ☐ #16 tapestry needle
- ☐ 5 (2¾ inches-long) aluminum wind chimes
- ☐ Invisible thread

INSTRUCTIONS

1 Cut hut from 7-count plastic canvas; cut sign from 10-count plastic canvas according to graphs. Cut two 19-hole x 3-hole pieces from 7-count plastic canvas for hut roof.

2 Stitch hut with yarn following graph, working uncoded areas on bird with lime Continental Stitches and uncoded area on flowers with crimson Continental Stitches. Continental Stitch roof pieces with forest yarn.

3 Continental Stitch uncoded background on sign with very light gray green #3 pearl cotton.

4 Overcast hut and sign following graphs, leaving roof edges on hut from dot to dot unstitched at this time.

5 Work embroidery on sign with black #8 pearl cotton. Work embroidery on hut with black #5 pearl cotton and white #3 pearl cotton.

6 Center sign above door on hut, placing center of sign one stitched row above door. Tack ends of sign to hut with invisible thread.

7 Using forest throughout, Whipstitch one short edge of each roof piece together, forming roof peak. Overcast remaining short edges and front edges. Whipstitch back edges to roof edges of hut, centering peak at top.

8 For each chime, thread a double strand of invisible thread through hole on chime and attach to hut where indicated on graph, keeping top edge of each chime 1¼ inches from adjacent bottom edge of hut.

9 For hanger, thread a 13-inch-long double strand of invisible thread through holes indicated on hut, leaving a loop that measures 4 inches above peak of roof. Secure ends by wrapping thread around plastic canvas and knotting off. ■

COLOR KEY

Plastic Canvas Yarn	Yards
■ Black #00	1
■ Red #01	4
■ Mint #24	2
▨ Baby green #26	1
▨ Forest #29	4
☐ White #41	1
▨ Yellow #57	5
Uncoded areas on bird are lime #22 Continental Stitches	1
Uncoded areas on flowers are crimson #42 Continental Stitches	1
#3 Pearl Cotton	
Uncoded background on sign is very light gray green #928 Continental Stitches	2
╱ Very light gray green #928 Overcasting	
╱ White Straight Stitch	1
○ White French Knot	
#5 Pearl Cotton	
╱ Black 310 Backstitch and Straight Stitch	3
#8 Pearl Cotton	
╱ Black #310 Backstitch and Straight Stitch	1
● Black #310 French Knot	
● Attach wind chime	
● Attach hanger	

Color numbers given are for Uniek Needloft plastic canvas yarn and DMC pearl cotton.

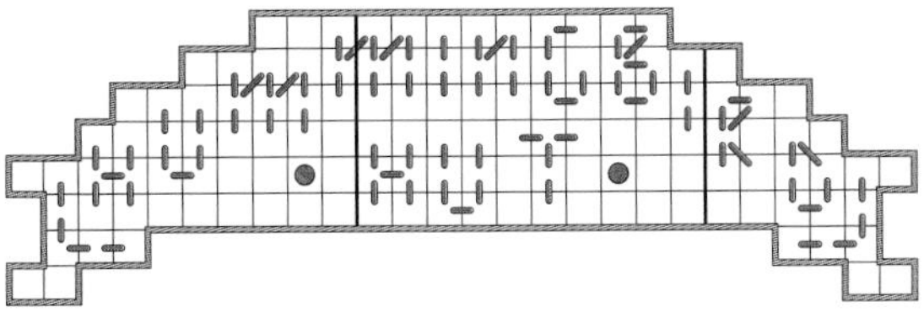

Hut Sign
26 holes x 8 holes
Cut 1 from 10-count
Stitch with #3 pearl cotton

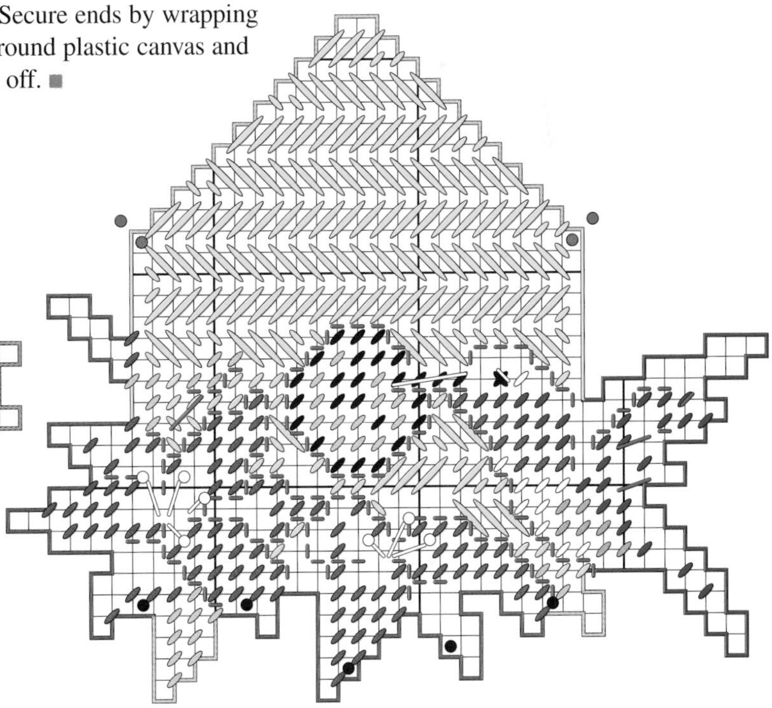

Hummingbird Hut
37 holes x 32 holes
Cut 1 from 7-count
Stitch with yarn

Frieda Froggy

With her bendable legs, this friendly frog can easily sit on top of a fence post or flower box, making a whimsical garden decoration!

Design by Lee Lindeman

TAKE NOTE

Skill Level: Intermediate

Finished Size: Approximately 10 inches W x 13 inches H

YOU'LL NEED

- 1 sheet 7-count plastic canvas
- Plastic canvas yarn as listed in color key
- 6-strand embroidery floss as listed in color key
- #16 tapestry needle
- 2 (15mm) light brown animal eyes
- 2 (³⁄₈-inch) white buttons
- Polyester fiberfill
- 15 inches ⅞-inch-wide pink sheer ribbon
- Hot-glue gun

CUTTING & STITCHING

1 Cut plastic canvas according to graphs. Cut four 3-hole x 15-hole pieces for upper arm, four 3-hole x 12-hole pieces for lower arm, four 3-hole x 13-hole pieces for upper leg and four 3-hole x 19-hole pieces for lower leg.

2 Stitch legs and arms with medium avocado Continental Stitches. Stitch all remaining pieces following graphs, working head back entirely in medium green avocado Continental Stitches. Reverse two hands and two feet before stitching.

3 When background stitching is completed, Backstitch mouth on head front with black embroidery floss and drop seat on body back with ecru embroidery floss.

ASSEMBLY

1 Using photo as a guide throughout assembly, glue eyes to head front. With one strand medium avocado yarn, sew buttons to drop seat on body back where indicated on graph.

2 Using medium avocado through step 8, Overcast bottom edges of head front and back, then Whipstitch wrong sides together around sides and top. Stuff with fiberfill.

3 Whipstitch wrong sides of body front and back together around sides and top. Stuff with fiberfill, then Whipstitch body bottom to front and back.

4 With wrong sides facing, Whipstitch two of each corresponding arm and leg pieces together along long side edges. Whipstitch one upper arm set to one lower arm set and one upper leg set to one lower leg set along short edge. Repeat with remaining arms and legs.

5 Whipstitch short edges on lower legs closed. Whipstitch short edges on upper arms closed.

6 Matching edges, Whipstitch wrong side of two foot pieces together, stuffing with fiberfill before closing. Repeat with remaining foot. Whipstitch top of legs to lower body front where indicated on graph. Glue feet to bottom edges of legs.

7 Matching edges, Whipstitch wrong sides of two hand pieces together, stuffing with fiberfill and leaving wrist edges open. Repeat with remaining hand.

8 Whipstitch wrist edges on hands to ends of lower arms. Glue upper arms to shoulder area on body back.

9 Glue neck of head over top of body. When glue is set, tie pink ribbon in a bow around neck, trimming ends as desired. ■

COLOR KEY

COLOR KEY	
Plastic Canvas Yarn	**Yards**
■ Medium avocado	100
▨ Light green	3
▨ Pink	1
6-Strand Embroidery Floss	
╱ Black Backstitch	1
╱ Ecru Backstitch	1
● Attach button	

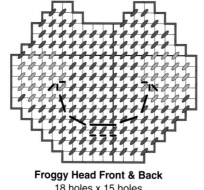

Froggy Head Front & Back
18 holes x 15 holes
Cut 2
Stitch front as graphed
Stitch back entirely with medium avocado Continental Stitches

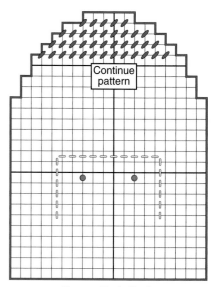

Froggy Body Back
19 holes x 25 holes
Cut 1

Froggy Foot
17 holes x 17 holes
Cut 4, reverse 2

Froggy Hand
13 holes x 15 holes
Cut 4, reverse 2

Continue
pattern

Attach leg   Attach leg

Froggy Body Bottom
15 holes x 7 holes
Cut 1

Froggy Body Front
19 holes x 25 holes
Cut 1

Country Time Wind Chime

Catch a summer breeze with this delightful cowbell wind chime.
Our holstein cow has found a shady spot under an apple tree!

Design by Lee Lindeman

TAKE NOTE

Skill Level: Intermediate

Finished Size: Approximately 7½ inches W x 13½ inches H x 4⅜ inches D

YOU'LL NEED

- ☐ 2 sheets regular 7-count plastic canvas
- ☐ ⅔ sheet stiff 7-count plastic canvas
- ☐ Worsted weight yarn as listed in color key
- ☐ 6-strand embroidery floss as listed in color key
- ☐ #16 tapestry needle
- ☐ Polyester fiberfill
- ☐ 2 (3mm) black beads
- ☐ Copper cow bells from Westrim Crafts: 2 (32mm), 6 (25mm) and 1 (¼ inch)
- ☐ 8 inches copper wire
- ☐ Wire clippers
- ☐ 3¾ inches leather cord
- ☐ 7 small screw eyes
- ☐ Needle-nose pliers
- ☐ Several jumbo crafts sticks
- ☐ Scissors
- ☐ 1¼-inch cork
- ☐ Bag tie with wire center
- ☐ 16 (10mm) wooden beads
- ☐ Acrylic paint: red, tan, brown and white
- ☐ Clear nail polish
- ☐ Paintbrush
- ☐ Small amount green and black felt
- ☐ Kitchen knife
- ☐ Hammer
- ☐ Hot-glue gun

PREPARATION

1 Using photo as a guide, make handles for basket from bag tie and insert into opposite sides of cork, gluing to secure.

2 Paint cork and handles with tan acrylic paint. When dry, paint woven slats on basket with brown.

3 For apples, paint wooden beads with red acrylic paint. When dry, coat apples with clear nail polish. Allow to dry.

4 Gently tap kitchen knife with a hammer to split 15 apples in half, leaving one whole apple.

5 Cut a small leaf from green felt and a small stem from black felt. Glue leaf and stem into hole of whole apple.

CUTTING & STITCHING

1 Cut base pieces from stiff plastic canvas; cut remaining pieces from regular plastic canvas according to graphs (pages 83 and 84).

2 Stitch pieces following graphs, reversing one of each piece before stitching.

3 Using black embroidery floss, Straight Stitch nostril on cows when background stitching is completed. Sew black beads to cow for eyes. Add a dot of white paint to beads for eye highlight.

4 Using medium brown throughout, Overcast bottom edges of tree trunks from dot to dot. Matching edges, Whipstitch wrong sides of tree trunk together along remaining edges. Stuff trunk with fiberfill.

5 Using medium avocado through step 6, Overcast tree left foliage pieces from dot to dot where indicated on right side of graph. Overcast tree middle foliage pieces between blue dots and between red dots. Overcast tree right foliage pieces from dot to dot where indicated on left side of graph.

6 With wrong sides together and matching edges, place a thin layer of fiberfill between top and bottom of base; Whipstitch together.

7 With wrong sides facing and using adjacent colors, Whipstitch mouth and neck edges of cow together, then Straight Stitch mouth around edge with black embroidery floss. Complete Whipstitching, stuffing with fiberfill before closing and leaving four small loops of pink yarn at bottom of udder if desired.

ASSEMBLY

1 Using photo as a guide throughout assembly, glue tree branches inside foliage. Gently spread roots of tree and glue to base.

2 Thread leather cord through hole at top of ¼-inch copper bell. Wrap cord around cow's neck, overlapping and gluing on backside of cow. Glue cow in place in front of tree.

3 Using wire cutters and needle-nose pliers and following Fig. 1 (page 84), cut 3½ inches copper wire to make hanger for top of wind chimes. Attach to holes indicated at top of center tree foliage.

4 For center hanger at bottom of base, screw one small screw eye into center bottom of base, gluing to secure.

5 Following Fig. 2 (page 84), cut 2½ inch-length copper wire for U-shaped hanger, adding 32mm copper bells before closing loops. Use remaining 2 inches for straight hanger, attach to U-shaped hanger and to center screw eye at bottom of base.

6 Attach 25mm copper bells to remaining screw eyes. Allowing 1½ inches to 2 inches between screw eyes, screw six screw eyes into bottom of base around center hanger, gluing to secure.

7 Glue half apples to both sides of tree foliage and to top of cork basket, placing whole apple on top of apples on basket. Glue basket to base. ∎

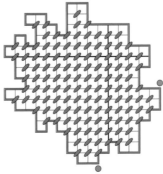

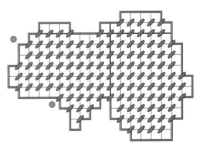

COLOR KEY

Worsted Weight Yarn	Yards
■ Medium avocado	124
■ Medium brown	40
□ White	20
■ Black	12
■ Pink	3
6-Strand Embroidery Floss	
✎ Black Straight Stitch	1
○ Attach hanger	

Tree Left Foliage
15 holes x 15 holes
Cut 2, reverse 1, from regular

Tree Right Foliage
18 holes x 12 holes
Cut 2, reverse 1, from regular

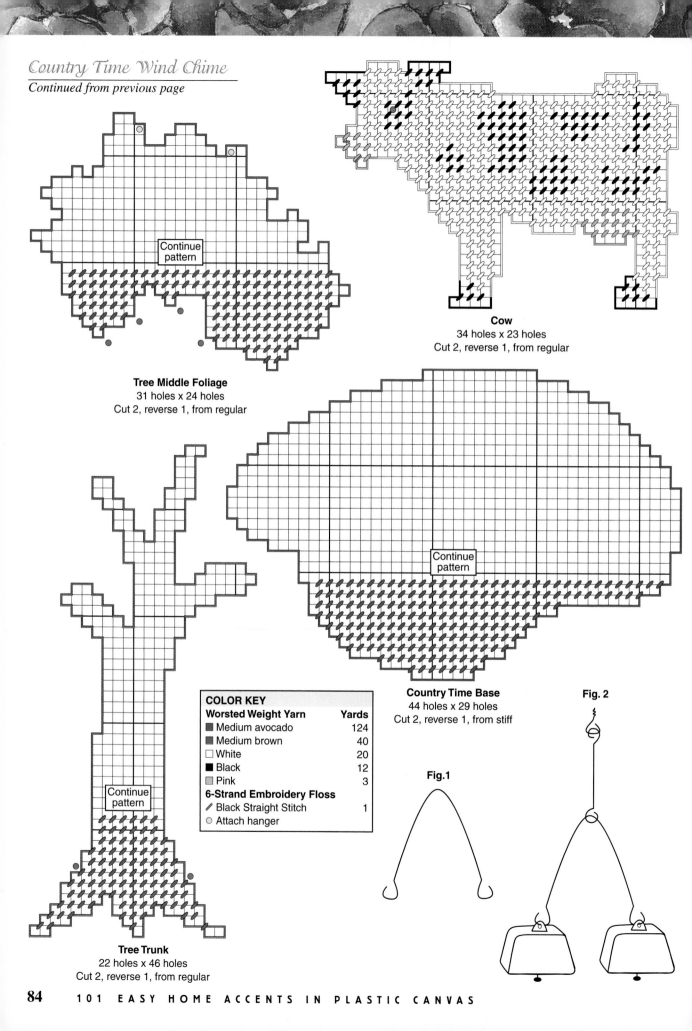

Cow
34 holes x 23 holes
Cut 2, reverse 1, from regular

Tree Middle Foliage
31 holes x 24 holes
Cut 2, reverse 1, from regular

Continue
pattern

Country Time Base
44 holes x 29 holes
Cut 2, reverse 1, from stiff

Continue
pattern

Continue
pattern

Fig. 2

Fig.1

COLOR KEY

Worsted Weight Yarn	Yards
■ Medium avocado	124
■ Medium brown	40
□ White	20
■ Black	12
■ Pink	3
6-Strand Embroidery Floss	
✎ Black Straight Stitch	1
○ Attach hanger	

Tree Trunk
22 holes x 46 holes
Cut 2, reverse 1, from regular

Butterfly Plant Poke
Stitch a pretty butterfly that won't flutter away!
Use it to dress up a favorite window box or flowerpot!

Design by Angie Arickx

TAKE NOTE

Skill Level: Beginner

Finished Size: Approximately 3½ inches W x 10 inches H

YOU'LL NEED

- ☐ Small amount black 7-count plastic canvas
- ☐ Uniek Needloft plastic canvas yarn as listed in color key
- ☐ #16 tapestry needle
- ☐ 9 inch (¼-inch-wide) dowel
- ☐ Pencil sharpener or pocket knife
- ☐ Hot-glue gun

INSTRUCTIONS

1 Cut plastic canvas according to graph, cutting away blue lines around antennae, leaving each antenna one bar wide. Leaving holes intact, carefully cut apart plastic canvas in center of piece between bottom part of body and lower wings at red lines.

2 Stitch and Overcast butterfly following graph. Do not Overcast antennae.

3 Sharpen one end of dowel with pencil sharpener or pocket knife. Glue butterfly to unsharpened end. ■

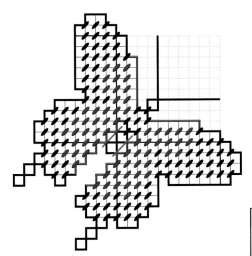

Plant Poke Butterfly
22 holes x 22 holes
Cut 1, cutting away blue lines
around antennae
Cut apart at red lines

COLOR KEY	
Plastic Canvas Yarn	**Yards**
■ Black #00	4
■ Royal #32	2
Color numbers given are for Uniek Needloft plastic canvas yarn.	

Butterfly Wind Chime

Capture the beauty of the monarch butterfly with this exquisite project.
Hang an assortment of chimes to add a lovely sound to your lovely project.

Design by Janelle Giese

TAKE NOTE

Skill Level: Beginner

Finished Size: 6 inches W x 4¼ inches H, excluding hanger and wind chimes

YOU'LL NEED

- ¼ sheet 7-count plastic canvas
- Small amount 10-count plastic canvas
- Uniek Needloft plastic canvas yarn as listed in color key
- DMC #3 pearl cotton as listed in color key
- #16 tapestry needle
- 5 (6mm) gold-tone steel wind chimes
- Invisible thread
- Thick white glue

INSTRUCTIONS

1 Cut butterfly wings from 7-count plastic canvas; cut butterfly body from 10-count plastic canvas according to graphs.

2 Stitch wings with yarn following graph, working uncoded areas with black Continental Stitches. Continental Stitch uncoded background on body with black #3 pearl cotton. Overcast pieces following graphs.

3 Work Backstitches and Straight Stitches with pearl cotton following graphs. Work French Knots on wings, wrapping white pearl cotton around needle two times and very light topaz pearl cotton around needle three times.

4 Use photo as a guide through step 7. For antennae, thread a 4-inch length of black pearl cotton through back of stitches on top of head. Bend ends upward, then use fingers to coat with glue. Allow to dry thoroughly. Trim ends to measure 1⅝ inches above head.

5 Place upper part of body over center of wing; tack in place with black pearl cotton.

6 Using invisible thread, attach chimes to butterfly where indicated on graph, keeping bottom edge of each chime 5 inches below bottom edge of wings. When attaching center chime, thread invisible thread through back of stitches on lower part of body.

7 For hanger, thread a 10-inch-long double strand of invisible thread through holes indicated on butterfly, leaving a loop that measures 4 inches above top edge of wings. Secure ends by wrapping thread around plastic canvas and knotting off. ∎

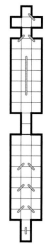

Wind Chime Butterfly Body
3 holes x 22 holes
Cut 1 from 10-count
Stitch with pearl cotton

COLOR KEY

Plastic Canvas Yarn	Yards
▨ Tangerine #11	3
■ Pumpkin #12	2
☐ White #41	1
▧ Yellow #57	2
Uncoded areas on wings are black #00 Continental Stitches	6
╱ Black #00 Overcasting	
#3 Pearl Cotton	
Uncoded background on body is black #310 Continental Stitches	6
╱ Black #310 Backstitch and Overcasting	
╱ White Backstitch and Straight Stitch	2
○ White French Knot	
○ Very light topaz #727 French Knot	1
● Attach wind chime	
● Attach hanger	

Color numbers given are for Uniek Needloft plastic canvas yarn and DMC pearl cotton.

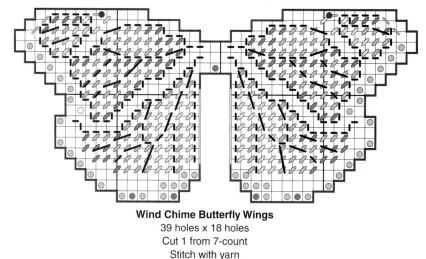

Wind Chime Butterfly Wings
39 holes x 18 holes
Cut 1 from 7-count
Stitch with yarn

Flower Box Door Chime

*Welcome guests into your home with this enchanting door chime
decorated with pretty silk flowers and a watering can!*

Design by Celia Lange Designs

TAKE NOTE

Skill Level: Intermediate

Finished Size: Approximately
6½ inches W x 15½ inches H

YOU'LL NEED

- ☐ 1 sheet 7-count plastic canvas
- ☐ Coats & Clark Red Heart Classic worsted weight yarn Art. E267 as listed in color key
- ☐ ⅛-inch-wide Plastic Canvas 7 Metallic Needlepoint Yarn by Rainbow Gallery as listed in color key
- ☐ #16 tapestry needle
- ☐ 5 (6mm) gold-tone steel wind chimes
- ☐ Assorted miniature silk flowers
- ☐ Miniature ivy leaves
- ☐ Iridescent spray pick
- ☐ Nylon fishing line
- ☐ Hot-glue gun

CUTTING & STITCHING

1 Cut plastic canvas according to graphs (this page and page 90). Cut one 11-hole x 1-hole piece for chime hanger. Chime hanger will remain unstitched.

2 Stitch remaining pieces following graphs, reversing one watering can before stitching. When background stitching is completed, work gold Backstitches on watering can pieces, wrapping Backstitches around edges.

3 Using skipper blue, Overcast top edge of each watering can from dot to dot, then Overcast each bottom edge. Whipstitch wrong sides together along all remaining edges, skipping edges with gold Backstitching. Overcast sprinkler heads with gold.

4 For flower box lining pieces, Overcast bottom edges from dot to dot with warm brown. Overcast top edges where indicated with paddy green. Whipstitch wrong sides together along remaining edges with adjacent colors.

5 Using black for flower box pieces throughout, Overcast bottom edges from dot to dot; Overcast top and inside edges. Whipstitch wrong sides together along remaining edges.

TWISTED CORD HANGER

1 To make twisted cord hanger, cut one 1½ yard length and one 1 yard length of black yarn.

2 Twist 1½ yard length until it begins to loop back on itself. Place both ends together, folding yarn in half; allow halves to twist around each other. Tie a knot in both ends, then tie a 2-inch hanging loop in center, leaving knot loose at this time.

3 Secure one end of remaining 1 yard length of black yarn; twist as in step 2. When yarn begins to loop back on itself, tie a knot in unsecured end.

4 Keeping twist in yarn, slip knotted end through loose knot of hanging loop to center of yarn. Tighten loop, place ends together and allow halves to twist around each other.

FINAL ASSEMBLY

1 Use photo as a guide throughout final assembly. Place lining inside flower box, then glue together along bottom edge to secure, but do not glue bottom edges of basket or lining shut.

2 Adjusting lengths of twisted cord hanger to hang evenly, insert center (shorter) strand into opening at top of flower box lining. Glue to secure.

3 Thread left strand of twisted cord hanger between watering can pieces, then glue this strand and right strand to flower box where indicated on graph. Glue watering can to cords.

4 Cut several 6- to 8-inch lengths of iridescent strands from pick. Thread strands through stitches on wrong side of both sprinkler heads and fold in center so two "water sprays" are formed by each strand.

5 Glue sprinkler heads to spout and to each other, making sure water is coming out the head and not leaking out the side.

6 Using nylon fishing line, attach one chime hanger by threading line through hole on chime, then wrapping around first two inside bars on left side of

hanger. Leave ½ inch between chime and hanger, then tie off securely at hanger.

7 Repeat with remaining four chimes, wrapping fishing line for each chime around two bars on hanger.

8 Insert chime hanger inside bottom of flower box lining; glue hanger to both sides of lining. Glue bottom edges of flower box closed, leaving center area between arrows open.

9 Glue ivy leaves to paddy green section of flower box lining, then glue flowers inside top edge of flower box. ■

COLOR KEY	
Worsted Weight Yarn	**Yards**
■ Black #12	21
■ Warm brown #336	17
■ Paddy green #686	8
■ Skipper blue #848	8
⅛-Inch Metallic Needlepoint Yarn	
☐ Gold #PC1	1
╱ Gold #PC1 Backstitch	
● Attach hanging cord	
Color numbers given are for Coats & Clark Red Heart Classic worsted weight yarn Art. E267 and Rainbow Gallery Plastic Canvas 7 Metallic Needlepoint Yarn.	

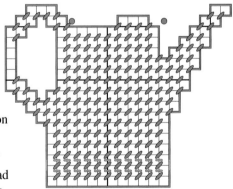

Watering Can
22 holes x 17 holes
Cut 2, reverse 1

Sprinkler Head
2 holes x 5 holes
Cut 2

Flower Box Door Chime

Continued from previous page

Continued from previous page

COLOR KEY	
Worsted Weight Yarn	**Yards**
■ Black #12	21
■ Warm brown #336	17
■ Paddy green #686	8
■ Skipper blue #848	8
⅛-Inch Metallic Needlepoint Yarn	
▢ Gold #PC1	1
⁄ Gold #PC1 Backstitch	
● Attach hanging cord	

Color numbers given are for Coats & Clark Red Heart Classic worsted weight yarn Art. E267 and Rainbow Gallery Plastic Canvas 7 Metallic Needlepoint Yarn.

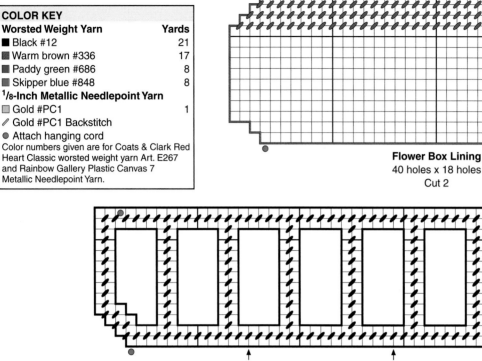

Continue pattern

Flower Box Lining
40 holes x 18 holes
Cut 2

Flower Box
44 holes x 13 holes
Cut 2

Tips & Techniques

To save money, yet maintain high-quality work on our 10-count plastic canvas projects, my husband and I purchase 4-ply worsted-weight yarn. We cut it into 18-inch lengths, then separated it into 2-ply. We use 2-ply for most of the stitching and 1-ply for detail. Our projects turn out beautifully while saving us plenty.
—*Cindy Cox, Pennsylvania*

I am limited for space for storing and organizing my completed projects, so I found and easy method to accomplish both.

I get sturdy boxes with lids from our local grocery store (free). I store and label each according to holiday. Christmas goes in one box, Easter in another, etc. When the holiday season approaches I have my crafts ready in a moment's time for selling.
—*Barbara Witte, Pennsylvania*

Instead of buying containers for my plastic canvas supplies, I collect and use tins. As they set around my home, the tins are pretty and practical!
—*Heather Monroe, Nevada*

Run the base of a 2-or 3-liter plastic drink bottom under hot water until the glue softens. Pull off the cap, then cut off the bottom inch of the bottle. Place a skein of yarn inside the bottle, thread it though the top, then put the cap back on. This will keep your yarn clean and the see-through bottle lets you see what color is inside.
—*Mrs. E. L. Daniel, Alabama*

To separate embroidery floss, just cut the length you'll need, then moisten it with a dampened sponge. The moist strands will separate easily and dry quickly for use.
—*Sue Wiener, Florida*

When using floss to stitch 10- or 14-count plastic canvas, I have found the ends to be too bulky to pull through the canvas comfortably. My solution: Cut a longer, single length of floss (6-strand for 10-count and

3-strand for 14-count) and thread one end of the floss through the needle until you reach the middle of the length. You now have the correct thickness to stitch with, but no extra ends to yank through the holes.
—*Cherie Marie Leck, North Carolina*

I like to keep extra sheets of plastic canvas on hand. I was having a problem keeping them flat and straight. Laying them in a box took up too much space and didn't always solve the problem of warped and crooked canvas. I also had to go through the entire stack when I needed a certain type or color. This was both time-consuming and costly.

I solved the problem by using an over-the-door hanger and old belt hanger. On each of the 10 individual hooks on the belt hanger, I hung different types of canvas by color. Now they are all divided and hang in plain sight. When I need one, I just snip it off and use.
—*A. Marie Connor, Illinois*

Chapter Five

Baskets & Containers

*Enjoy this collection of projects as you stitch them for
one-of-a-kind home accents, or for giving two-gifts-in-one
to family and friends! You'll find a pleasing selection of seasonal,
holiday and all-occasion carry-alls in this vibrant chapter.*

Country Hearts & Bears

Delight a shut-in with this darling basket filled with fruit, cookies and other tasty tidbits! It's sure to brighten her day!

Photo on page 91

Designs by Judy Collishaw

TAKE NOTE

Skill Level: Beginner

Finished Size:

Basket: 8 inches W x 11¾ inches H x 8 inches D

Plant Poke: 3⅞ inches W x 12 inches H

YOU'LL NEED

Basket

- ☐ 3 artist-size sheets stiff 7-count plastic canvas
- ☐ 1½ sheets regular 7-count plastic canvas
- ☐ Worsted weight yarn as listed in color key
- ☐ #16 tapestry needle
- ☐ 10 (½-inch) natural buttons
- ☐ 2 (½-inch) dark brown buttons

Plant Poke

- ☐ ⅓ sheet 10-count plastic canvas
- ☐ Sport weight yarn as listed in color key
- ☐ #18 tapestry needle
- ☐ 2 (¼-inch) natural buttons
- ☐ 12 inches (⅛-inch) dowel

Both Projects

- ☐ Small amount natural raffia
- ☐ Low-temperature glue gun

BASKET

CUTTING & STITCHING

1 Cut sides, bottom, corners and handle from 7-count stiff plastic canvas; cut bear pieces and hearts from 7-count regular plastic canvas according to graphs (pages 93, 94 and 105). Basket bottom will remain unstitched.

2 Stitch remaining pieces with worsted weight yarn following graphs, working sides and handle with ivory first, then filling in with medium blue. Work noses with black vertical stitches first, then horizontal stitches.

3 When background stitching is completed, work black Backstitches on bear heads. Following graphs throughout, Overcast hearts and standing bear pieces.

4 Overcast edges on sitting bears except between dots on both sides of bears. Overcast around uneven edges of paws from dot to dot. Whipstitch paws to bear sides from dot to dot along remaining edges.

ASSEMBLY

1 Use photo as a guide throughout assembly. Using medium blue through step 5, Whipstitch corners to sides, then Whipstitch corners and sides to unstitched basket bottom.

2 Overcast long edges of handles, then Overcast top edges of sides, Whipstitching short edges of handles to opposite sides of basket where indicated on graph from blue dot to blue dot.

3 Center and glue sitting bears to basket sides below handles. Glue striped hearts between paws to bear tummies.

4 For each standing bear, glue one right leg behind left leg. Where indicated on graphs, sew one button and one arm to bear with two sturdy strands of natural raffia; tie raffia in a knot on button front and trim ends.

5 Center and glue standing bears to remaining basket sides, gluing one polka-dot heart behind each hand.

6 Using two sturdy strands of natural raffia sew one ½-inch natural button to each button heart; tie raffia in a knot on button front and trim ends. Glue two hearts to each corner and one to each end of handle above sitting bears.

PLANT POKE

1 Cut sitting bear pieces, striped heart and button hearts from 10-count plastic canvas according to graphs (pages 94 and 105).

2 Stitch pieces with sport weight yarn following graphs, working nose with black vertical stitches first, then horizontal stitches.

3 Following graphs, Overcast edges on sitting bear except between dots on both sides of bear. Overcast around uneven edges of paws from dot to dot. Whipstitch paws to bear sides from dot to dot along remaining edges.

4 Overcast hearts with red.

5 Center one ¼-inch natural button on each button heart and sew in place with natural raffia; tie raffia in a knot on button front and trim ends to ⅝ inch.

6 Glue striped heart to bear tummy between paws. Center and glue dowel to backside of bear. Glue button hearts to dowel below bear. ∎

Button Heart
9 holes x 9 holes
Cut 10 from 7-count regular
Stitch with worsted weight yarn
Cut 2 from 10-count
Stitch with sport weight yarn

Striped Heart
13 holes x 11 holes
Cut 2 from 7-count regular
Stitch with worsted weight yarn
Cut 1 from 10-count
Stitch with sport weight yarn

COLOR KEY
BASKET

Worsted Weight Yarn	Yards
Medium blue	60
Ivory	36
Mahogany	23
Red	17
Tan	11
Black	1
Rust	1
Rose	1
Black Backstitch	
Ivory French Knot	
Attach button and arm	

Basket Side
41 holes x 41 holes
Cut 4 from 7-count stiff
Stitch with worsted weight yarn

Basket Corner
5 holes x 41 holes
Cut 4 from 7-count stiff
Stitch with worsted weight yarn

Standing Bear Arm
6 holes x 12 holes
Cut 2 from 7-count clear
Stitch with worsted weight yarn

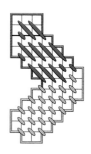

Standing Bear Right Leg
7 holes x 12 holes
Cut 2 from 7-count clear
Stitch with worsted weight yarn

Standing Bear
28 holes x 33 holes
Cut 2 from 7-count clear
Stitch with worsted weight yarn

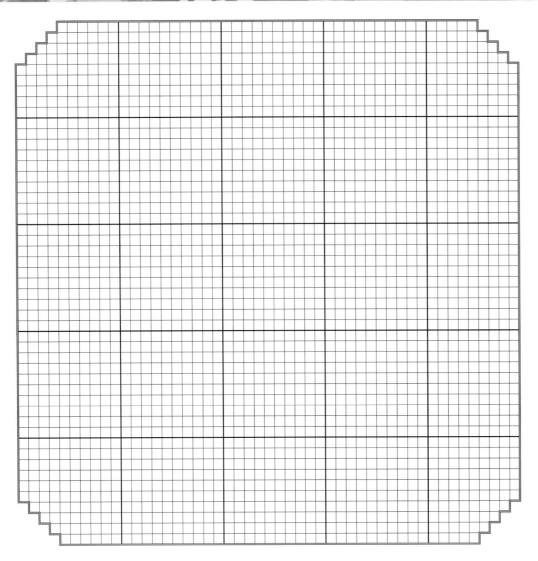

Basket Bottom
49 holes x 49 holes
Cut 1 from 7-count stiff
Do not stitch

COLOR KEY
BASKET

Worsted Weight Yarn	Yards
■ Medium blue	60
□ Ivory	36
■ Mahogany	23
■ Red	17
■ Tan	11
■ Black	1
■ Rust	1
■ Rose	1
╱ Black Backstitch	
○ Ivory French Knot	
● Attach button and arm	

COLOR KEY
PLANT POKE

Sport Weight Yarn	Yards
■ Mahogany	6
■ Red	6
■ Tan	3
□ Ivory	1
■ Black	1
■ Rust	1
■ Rose	1
╱ Black Backstitch	

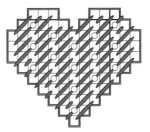

Polka Dot Heart
13 holes x 11 holes
Cut 2 from 7-count clear
Stitch with worsted weight yarn

Basket Handle
9 holes x 97 holes
Cut 1 from 7-count stiff
Stitch with worsted weight yarn

Graphs continued on page 105

Autumn Leaves

Filled with fresh-from-the-oven rolls or tasty nuts, this colorful basket serves a practical purpose while adding a colorful touch to your Thanksgiving table.

Design by Lee Lindeman

TAKE NOTE

Skill Level: Beginner

Finished Size: Approximately 12¼ inches H x 10 inches in diameter

YOU'LL NEED

- ☐ 3 sheets 7-count plastic canvas
- ☐ Worsted weight yarn as listed in color key
- ☐ #16 tapestry needle
- ☐ 10 small twigs
- ☐ Round basket with handle approximately 12 inches H x 8 inches in diameter
- ☐ 5 brown chenille stems
- ☐ Pencil
- ☐ 1 yard 1½-inch-wide natural fabric ribbon
- ☐ Hot-glue gun

INSTRUCTIONS

1 Cut plastic canvas according to graphs (this page and page 105).

2 Continental Stitch leaves following graphs, working one large leaf with yellow as graphed and one with orange.

3 Work one small leaf A with yellow as graphed, one with burnt orange and one with medium copper. Work four small leaves B with burnt orange as graphed and one with gold.

4 Overcast leaves with adjacent colors.

5 Using photo as a guide through step 7, glue one twig to center bottom of each leaf, then glue leaves around rim of basket.

6 Wind chenille stems around pencil so they resemble coiled vines; glue all stems to same handle side just above basket rim.

7 Tie natural fabric ribbon in a bow around handle, covering glued ends of chenille stems; trim ribbon ends. Glue bow to secure. ◼

COLOR KEY	
Worsted Weight Yarn	**Yards**
◼ Burnt orange	20
☐ Bright yellow	11
Orange	11
Gold	5
Medium copper	4

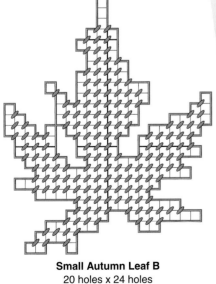

Small Autumn Leaf B
20 holes x 24 holes
Cut 5
Stitch 4 as graphed
Stitch 1 with gold

Graphs continued on page 105

Baby Photo Bank

Start saving for your youngster's future by putting your spare change in this musical bank.

Design by Janelle Marie Giese

TAKE NOTE

Skill Level: Beginner

Finished Size: 5¾ inches W x 7½ inches H x 2¾ inches D

YOU'LL NEED

- [ ] 1 artist-size sheet 7-count plastic canvas
- [ ] Chenille yarn as listed in color key
- [ ] Kreinik ⅛-inch Ribbon as listed in color key
- [ ] DMC #5 pearl cotton as listed in color key
- [ ] DMC 6-strand embroidery floss: #745 light pale yellow
- [ ] #16 tapestry needle
- [ ] 18 inches ⅛-inch (4mm) twisted ivory satin cording
- [ ] 80 (3mm) white pearl beads
- [ ] Beading needle
- [ ] Coin activated musical movement
- [ ] Thick white glue

INSTRUCTIONS

1 Cut plastic canvas according to graphs (this page and page 102). Cut two 14-hole x 8-hole pieces and two 32-hole x 8-hole pieces for lid lips, one 34-hole x 46-hole piece for frame back and one 34-hole x 16-hole piece for bank base. Lid lips, frame back and bank base will remain unstitched.

2 Following graphs throughout, Scotch Stitch bank front with yellow, then work Woven Scotch Stitch (Fig. 1, page 102) with star yellow where indicated on graph. *Note: Ribbon will twist less if woven under one strand of yarn at a time.*

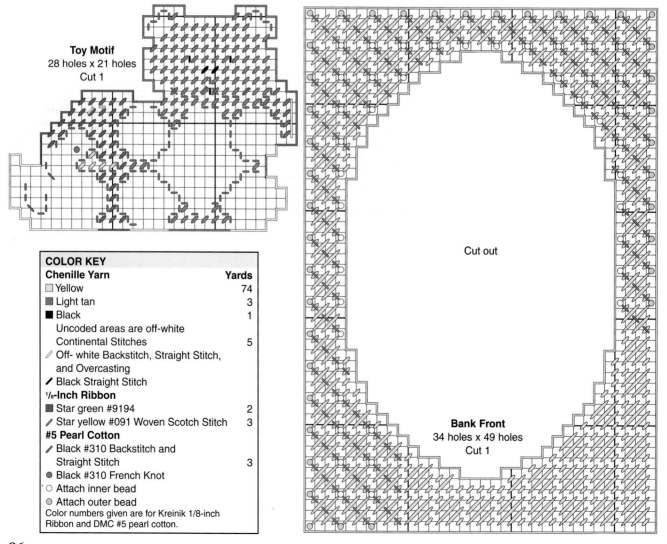

Toy Motif
28 holes x 21 holes
Cut 1

COLOR KEY	
Chenille Yarn	**Yards**
☐ Yellow	74
▨ Light tan	3
■ Black	1
Uncoded areas are off-white Continental Stitches	5
╱ Off-white Backstitch, Straight Stitch, and Overcasting	
╱ Black Straight Stitch	
⅛-Inch Ribbon	
■ Star green #9194	2
╱ Star yellow #091 Woven Scotch Stitch	3
#5 Pearl Cotton	
╱ Black #310 Backstitch and Straight Stitch	3
● Black #310 French Knot	
○ Attach inner bead	
◉ Attach outer bead	
Color numbers given are for Kreinik 1/8-inch Ribbon and DMC #5 pearl cotton.	

Bank Front
34 holes x 49 holes
Cut 1

Cut out

3 Overcast opening edges of front with yellow. Using two strands light pale yellow floss and beading needle, attach inner beads to front where indicated on graph. Glue ivory satin cording to edge of photo opening, joining at lower right corner.

4 Continental Stitch lid top, leaving the blue Whipstitch lines unworked at this time. Stitch sides, back and toy motif, working uncoded areas with off-white Continental Stitches.

5 Overcast toy motif following graph. Work black chenille yarn Straight Stitches, then complete embroidery with black pearl cotton.

6 Using yellow through step 8, Whipstitch bottom edges of sides to short edges of base. Making sure bottom edges are even, place frame back behind front, then Whipstitch to bottom and sides through all three thicknesses. *Note: Front will be three holes higher than sides and back.*

7 Following step 3, attach outer pearls along side edges of front where indicated on graph. With yellow, Whipstitch frame back to sides and bottom. Over-

cast remaining edges of assembled bank. Following graph, attach outer pearls along top edge of front.

8 Whipstitch 8-hole edges of large lid lips to small lid lips, then Whipstitch lid lips to lid top along blue Whipstitch lines. Overcast all remaining edges of lid top and lid lips. Glue musical movement in opening of lid top.

9 Glue toy motif to lower right corner of bank, making sure bottom edges are even. Slide photo into frame and attach near top as desired. Place lid on top with extended edge to the back. ∎

Graphs continued on page 102

Spools & Buttons

A colorful box with matching needle holder is just the right size for holding all your stitching supplies!

Designs by Laura Scott

TAKE NOTE

Skill Level: Intermediate

Finished Size:

Box: 6½ inches W x 3⅞ inches H x 5½ inches D

Needle Case: 3¼ inches W x 2⅞ inches H

YOU'LL NEED

- □ 1½ sheets Darice Ultra Stiff 7-count plastic canvas
- □ Uniek Needloft plastic canvas yarn as listed in color key
- □ #16 tapestry needle
- □ ½-inch buttons: 1 each red, purple, blue and green
- □ ⅜-inch buttons: 4 red, 3 purple, 5 blue and 4 green
- □ White sewing thread and sewing needle
- □ 3 (8-inch x 11-inch) pieces white felt
- □ Hot-glue gun

BOX

1 Cut plastic canvas according to graphs. Cut two 41-hole x 24-hole pieces for box front and back, two 35-hole x 24-hole pieces for box sides, one 41-hole x 35-hole piece for box bottom and one 34-hole x 20-hole piece for vertical divider. Box bottom and both dividers will remain unstitched.

2 Using box bottom, box sides and lid top as templates, cut felt for lining, cutting slightly smaller than plastic canvas pieces. Set aside.

3 Using camel, Continental Stitch box front, back and sides. Stitch lid top and lid sides following graphs, working uncoded areas with white Continental Stitches.

4 When background stitching is completed, Straight Stitch "thread" on spools and Backstitch around spools, using colors to match thread on spools.

5 Using sewing needle and white thread and referring to photo for color sequence, sew ½-inch buttons to lid top where indicated on graphs; sew ⅜-inch buttons to lid sides where graphed, attaching a red, purple, blue and green button to each long side and a red, green and blue button to each short side.

6 Using camel throughout, Whipstitch box front, back and sides together, then Whipstitch front, back and sides to box bottom; Overcast top edges. Whipstitch lid long sides to lid short sides, then Whipstitch sides to lid top; Overcast bottom edges.

Fig. 1

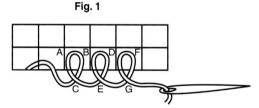

Buttonhole Stitch
Bring needle up at A, down at B, through loop at C, pulling tight, down at D, through loop at E, pulling tight, down at F, through loop at G, pulling tight, etc.

COLOR KEY	
Plastic Canvas Yarn	**Yards**
■ Camel #43	73
Uncoded areas are white #41	
Continental Stitches	34
╱ Red #01 Backstitch and Straight Stitch	3
╱ Christmas green #28 Backstitch and Straight Stitch	2
╱ Purple #46 Backstitch and Straight Stitch	2
╱ Dark royal #48 Backstitch and Straight Stitch	2
╱ Yellow #57 Backstitch and Straight Stitch	2
○ Attach ½-inch button	
○ Attach ⅜-inch button	
X Attach yarn for closing	
Color numbers given are for Uniek Needloft plastic canvas yarn.	

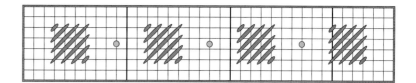

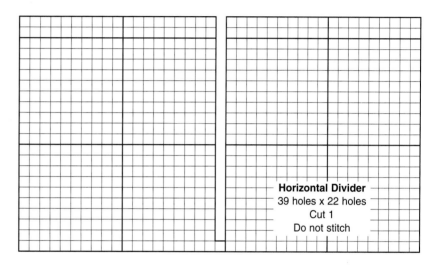

Lid Short Side
36 holes x 7 holes
Cut 2

Lid Long Side
42 holes x 7 holes
Cut 2

Horizontal Divider
39 holes x 22 holes
Cut 1
Do not stitch

7 Slide vertical divider into horizontal divider slot. Tack in place with yarn or glue to secure.

8 Glue felt lining pieces to underside of box lid and inside of box. Insert divider.

NEEDLE CASE

1 Cut needle case front according to graph. Cut one 20-hole x 18-hole piece for needle case back.

2 Using plastic canvas as templates, cut two pieces of felt for lining, cutting them slightly smaller than front and back. Set aside.

3 Stitch front according to graph, working uncoded areas with white Continental Stitches.

4 When background stitching is completed, Straight Stitch thread on spool, then Backstitch around spool with red. Continental Stitch back with camel.

5 Using camel and Buttonhole Stitch (Fig. 1) and with wrong sides together, join front and back along left-hand side of front. Work all remaining edges with a Buttonhole Stitch.

6 Using sewing needle and thread, sew blue and purple ⅜-inch buttons to front where indicated on graph. Glue felt to wrong sides of plastic canvas for lining.

7 Cut 12-inch length of camel yarn. Thread through both pieces where indicated on graph. To close needle case, tie yarn ends in a bow. ▪

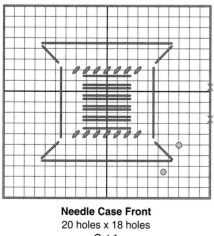

Needle Case Front
20 holes x 18 holes
Cut 1

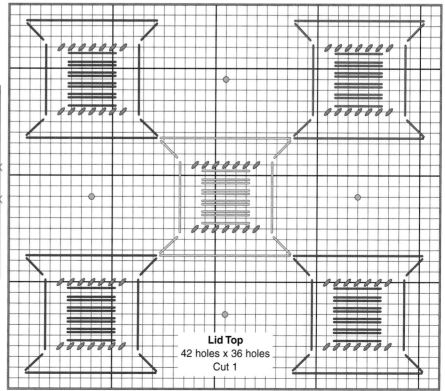

Lid Top
42 holes x 36 holes
Cut 1

Bunny & Chick Mini Bags

Filled with jelly beans, chocolate eggs and other treats, these cute bags make delightful favors for an Easter luncheon.

Designs by Celia Lange Designs

TAKE NOTE

Skill Level: Beginner

Finished Size:

Chick Bag: 4¼ inches W x 6½ inches H x 3½ inches D

Bunny Bag: 4¼ inches W x 6½ inches H x 3½ inches D

YOU'LL NEED

- ☐ 2 sheets Darice Ultra Stiff 7-count plastic canvas
- ☐ Coats & Clark Red Heart Classic worsted weight yarn Art. E267 as listed in color key
- ☐ DMC #3 pearl cotton as listed in color key
- ☐ #16 tapestry needle
- ☐ 4 (15mm) oval movable eyes
- ☐ Assorted small silk flowers and leaves
- ☐ Small amount green floral tape
- ☐ Hot-glue gun

INSTRUCTIONS

1 Cut plastic canvas according to graphs (this page and pages 101 and 102). Cut one 25-hole x17-hole piece for each bag bottom.

2 Continental Stitch chick bag bottom with paddy green and bunny bag bottom with true blue. Work chick bag front, back, sides and handles as graphed. Work bunny bag front, back, sides and handles replacing paddy green with true blue and emerald green with light periwinkle.

3 Stitch remaining pieces following graphs, working uncoded areas on chick and bunny pieces with off-white Continental Stitches.

4 Overcast chick pieces, bunny pieces and handles following graphs. Work pale rose Straight Stitches and black pearl cotton Backstitches when background stitching and Overcasting are completed.

5 Using paddy green for chick bag and true blue for bunny bag, Whipstitch corresponding bag fronts and backs to bag sides, then Whipstitch bag fronts, backs and sides to bag bottoms. Overcast top edges. Center and glue handles inside bag fronts and backs.

6 Using photo as a guide through step 8, arrange a small bouquet of flowers and leaves for both bags. Wrap stems with floral tape, cutting off excess stems.

7 Keeping bottom edges even, center and glue chick body to bag front. Glue head to body, then glue eyes and beak to head. Glue wings and flowers to body front, making sure bottom edges are even.

8 Keeping bottom edges even, center and glue bunny body to bag front. Glue head to body, then glue eyes to head and ear tip to short ear. Glue arms and flowers to body front, making sure bottom edges are even. ■

COLOR KEY

BUNNY BAG

Worsted Weight Yarn	Yards
☐ Emerald green #676	4
☐ Pale rose #755	1
True blue #822	38
Light periwinkle #827	13
Uncoded areas are off-white #3 Continental Stitches	13
∕ Off-white #3 Overcasting	
∕ Pale rose #755 Straight Stitch	

#3 Pearl Cotton

∕ Black #310 Backstitch	

Color numbers given are for Coats & Clark Red Heart Classic worsted weight yarn Art. E267 and DMC #3 pearl cotton.

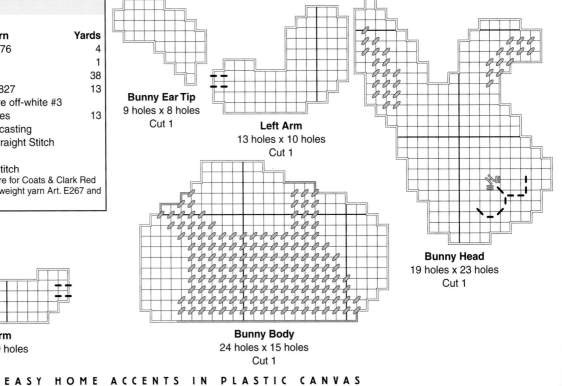

Bunny Ear Tip
9 holes x 8 holes
Cut 1

Left Arm
13 holes x 10 holes
Cut 1

Bunny Head
19 holes x 23 holes
Cut 1

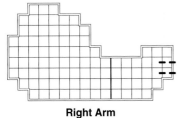

Right Arm
16 holes x 9 holes
Cut 1

Bunny Body
24 holes x 15 holes
Cut 1

Chick Body
24 holes x 15 holes
Cut 1

Chick Head
14 holes x 20 holes
Cut 1

Chick Beak
5 holes x 6 holes
Cut 1

Right Wing
16 holes x 10 holes
Cut 1

Left Wing
16 holes x 10 holes
Cut 1

Bunny & Chick Mini Bags
Continued from previous page

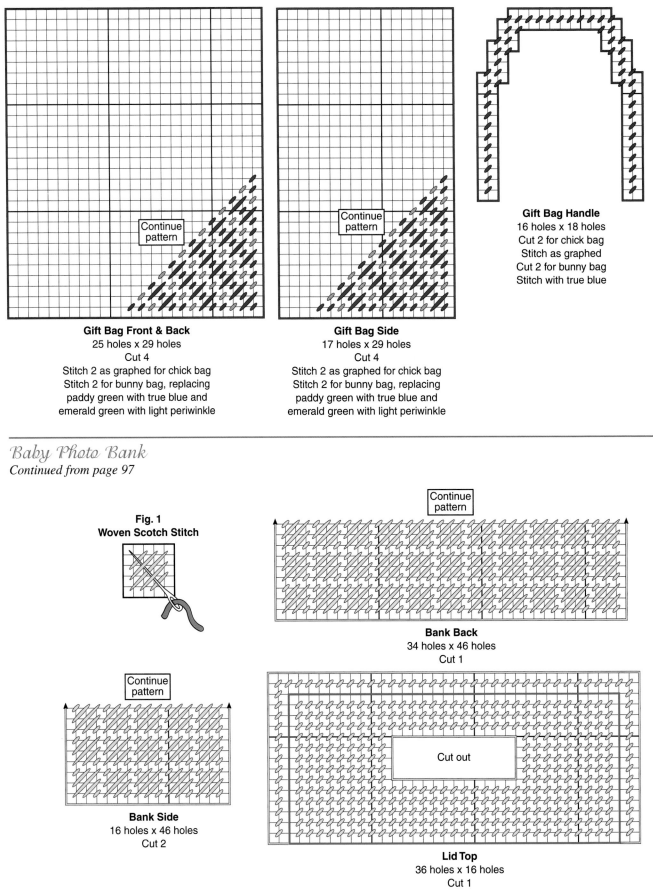

Gift Bag Handle
16 holes x 18 holes
Cut 2 for chick bag
Stitch as graphed
Cut 2 for bunny bag
Stitch with true blue

Gift Bag Front & Back
25 holes x 29 holes
Cut 4
Stitch 2 as graphed for chick bag
Stitch 2 for bunny bag, replacing
paddy green with true blue and
emerald green with light periwinkle

Gift Bag Side
17 holes x 29 holes
Cut 4
Stitch 2 as graphed for chick bag
Stitch 2 for bunny bag, replacing
paddy green with true blue and
emerald green with light periwinkle

Baby Photo Bank
Continued from page 97

Fig. 1
Woven Scotch Stitch

Bank Back
34 holes x 46 holes
Cut 1

Bank Side
16 holes x 46 holes
Cut 2

Cut out

Lid Top
36 holes x 16 holes
Cut 1

Peek-a-Boo Bunnies Basket

Delight your little one by stitching him or her this sweet basket for hunting Easter eggs!

Design by Angie Arickx

TAKE NOTE

Skill Level: Beginner

Finished Size: 7½ inches H x 5½ inches in diameter

YOU'LL NEED

- ☐ 1 sheet Darice Ultra Stiff 7-count plastic canvas
- ☐ 5-inch plastic canvas hexagon by Darice
- ☐ Uniek Needloft plastic canvas yarn as listed in color key
- ☐ #16 tapestry needle
- ☐ Hot-glue gun

INSTRUCTIONS

1 Cut plastic canvas according to graphs (page 104).

2 Stitch pieces following graphs, working uncoded areas with white Continental Stitches. Do not stitch plastic canvas hexagon which is basket bottom.

3 Overcast paws with white; Overcast heads with pink and white following graph. Using tan throughout, Overcast handle and top edges of basket sides. Whipstitch sides together, then Whipstitch sides to unstitched basket bottom.

4 Using photo as a guide, glue bunny heads and paws to top edges of basket sides. Glue handle ends inside basket to opposite corners. ■

Graphs on page 104

Peek-a-Boo Bunnies Basket
Continued from previous page

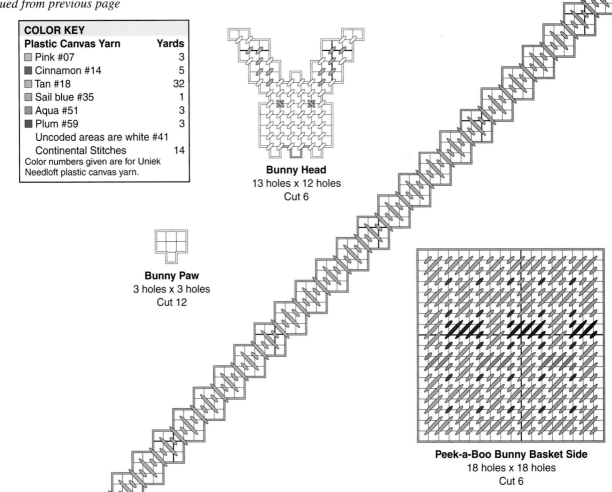

COLOR KEY	
Plastic Canvas Yarn	**Yards**
Pink #07	3
Cinnamon #14	5
Tan #18	32
Sail blue #35	1
Aqua #51	3
Plum #59	3
Uncoded areas are white #41	
Continental Stitches	14
Color numbers given are for Uniek Needloft plastic canvas yarn.	

Bunny Head
13 holes x 12 holes
Cut 6

Bunny Paw
3 holes x 3 holes
Cut 12

Peek-a-Boo Bunny Basket Side
18 holes x 18 holes
Cut 6

Peek-a-Boo Basket Handle
63 holes x 63 holes
Cut 1

Tips & Techniques

Before I start cutting plastic canvas for a project, I count the holes or bars in any large, straight areas on the graph, and make a notation of the measurement beside that portion of the graph. This makes counting and cutting a project much easier for me.

—*Wilma Shay, Texas*

Before you throw away that old pair of rubber gloves, cut off the tops and cut them into 2½-inch squares. These are ideal for pulling slippery needles through tight spots when stitching.

—*Wilma Shay, Texas*

If I'm working on a project that uses both 7- and 10-count plastic canvas and I need the same color of yarn for both sizes, I just separate the 4-ply yarn and use a ply or two on the 10-count plastic canvas. It saves me time and money.

—*Juanita Whalen, Ohio*

In the last few years I have gotten so deep into plastic canvas that I have converted an extra bedroom into my "craft office." One trick I learned was using a Sharpie permanent marker to draw the outline of a piece on the plastic canvas before cutting it. After cutting, I simply use old rags and rubbing alcohol to remove all traces of the marker.

—*Donna Hare, Florida*

I am a smoker. In order to keep my projects from staining or smelling like smoke, I put them in a sealable box or bag with a fabric softener sheet.

—*Paula LaFramboise, Vermont*

Country Hearts & Bears

Continued from page 94

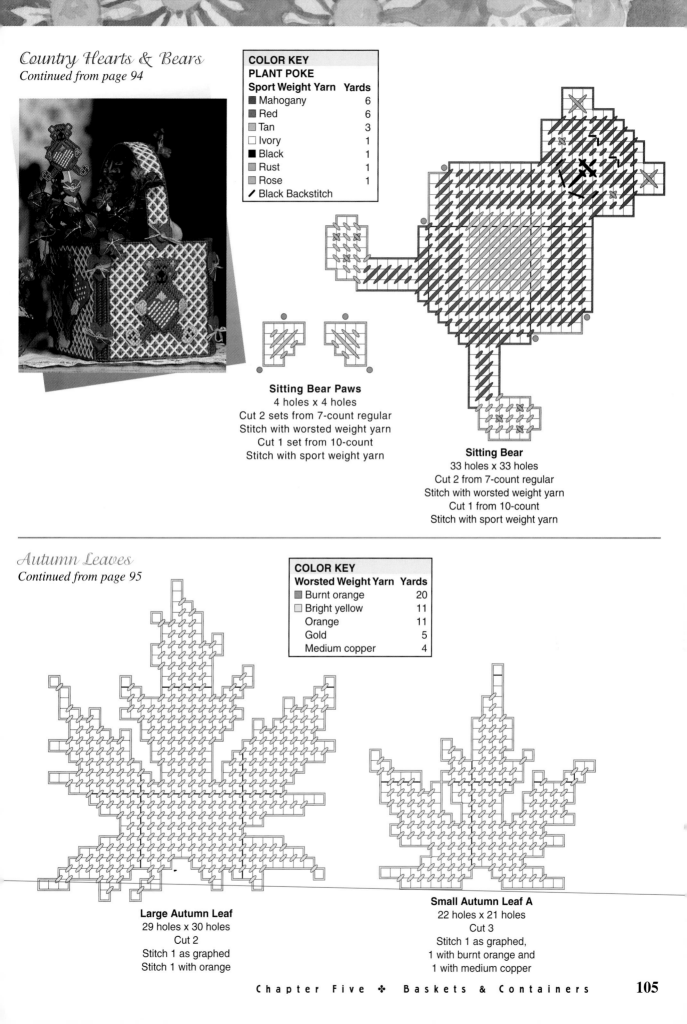

COLOR KEY	
PLANT POKE	
Sport Weight Yarn	**Yards**
■ Mahogany	6
■ Red	6
■ Tan	3
□ Ivory	1
■ Black	1
■ Rust	1
■ Rose	1
✎ Black Backstitch	

Sitting Bear Paws
4 holes x 4 holes
Cut 2 sets from 7-count regular
Stitch with worsted weight yarn
Cut 1 set from 10-count
Stitch with sport weight yarn

Sitting Bear
33 holes x 33 holes
Cut 2 from 7-count regular
Stitch with worsted weight yarn
Cut 1 from 10-count
Stitch with sport weight yarn

Autumn Leaves

Continued from page 95

COLOR KEY	
Worsted Weight Yarn	**Yards**
■ Burnt orange	20
□ Bright yellow	11
Orange	11
Gold	5
Medium copper	4

Large Autumn Leaf
29 holes x 30 holes
Cut 2
Stitch 1 as graphed
Stitch 1 with orange

Small Autumn Leaf A
22 holes x 21 holes
Cut 3
Stitch 1 as graphed,
1 with burnt orange and
1 with medium copper

Chapter Five ❖ Baskets & Containers   **105**

Turkey Basket

Friends and family will look forward to seeing this
festive decoration year after year at Thanksgiving dinner!

Design by Lee Lindeman

TAKE NOTE

Skill Level: Beginner

Finished Size: $9\frac{7}{8}$ inches W x $10\frac{1}{2}$ inches H x $17\frac{1}{2}$ inches L

YOU'LL NEED

- $4\frac{1}{2}$ sheets 7-count plastic canvas
- Worsted weight yarn as listed in color key
- #16 tapestry needle
- Small amount polyester fiberfill
- Oval basket with handle approximately 8 inches W x 12 inches H x 110 $\frac{3}{4}$ inches D
- 2 (12mm) brown crystal eyes from Westrim Crafts
- Small amount yellow craft foam or felt
- 2 yards 2-inch-wide coordinating ribbon
- Hot-glue gun

INSTRUCTIONS

1 Cut plastic canvas according to graphs (this page and page 108).

2 Stitch pieces following graphs, reversing two wings and one head before stitching and working uncoded areas with brown Continental Stitches.

3 With bright yellow, Overcast beaks from dot to dot. With wrong sides together, Whipstitch remaining edges of head pieces together with cherry red and bright yellow, stuffing with fiberfill before closing.

4 Cut small triangles from craft foam or felt to fit open areas of beak. Glue in place.

5 Using photo as a guide through step 9, slip neck part of head onto one basket end; glue to secure.

6 Whipstitch wrong sides of tail pieces together with adjacent colors. Glue to opposite end of basket. For each wing, matching edges, Whipstitch wrong sides of two wing pieces together with adjacent colors. Glue one wing to each basket side.

7 For wattle, cut a 12-inch length of cherry red yarn. Tie ends together in a knot, forming a large circle. Loop circle over index fingers of both hands. Twist fingers in opposite directions, twisting yarn until it begins to loop back on itself. Place both loops on one index finger, folding yarn in half; allow halves to twist around each other.

8 Measuring from folded end, knot twisted yarn at desired length. Glue knotted end of wattle above center of beak, allowing folded end to drop down side of beak.

9 Cut ribbon in half and tie both lengths in a bow. Glue bows to rim of basket at neck sides. ■

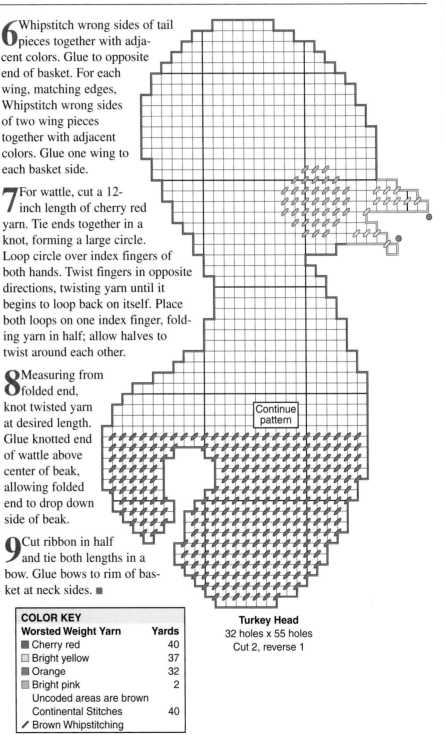

Turkey Head
32 holes x 55 holes
Cut 2, reverse 1

Continue pattern

COLOR KEY	
Worsted Weight Yarn	**Yards**
■ Cherry red	40
□ Bright yellow	37
■ Orange	32
▨ Bright pink	2
Uncoded areas are brown Continental Stitches	40
⁄ Brown Whipstitching	

Turkey Basket
Continued from page 106

Continued from page 106

COLOR KEY	
Worsted Weight Yarn	**Yards**
■ Cherry red	40
□ Bright yellow	37
■ Orange	32
▨ Bright pink	2
Uncoded areas are brown	
Continental Stitches	40
╱ Brown Whipstitching	

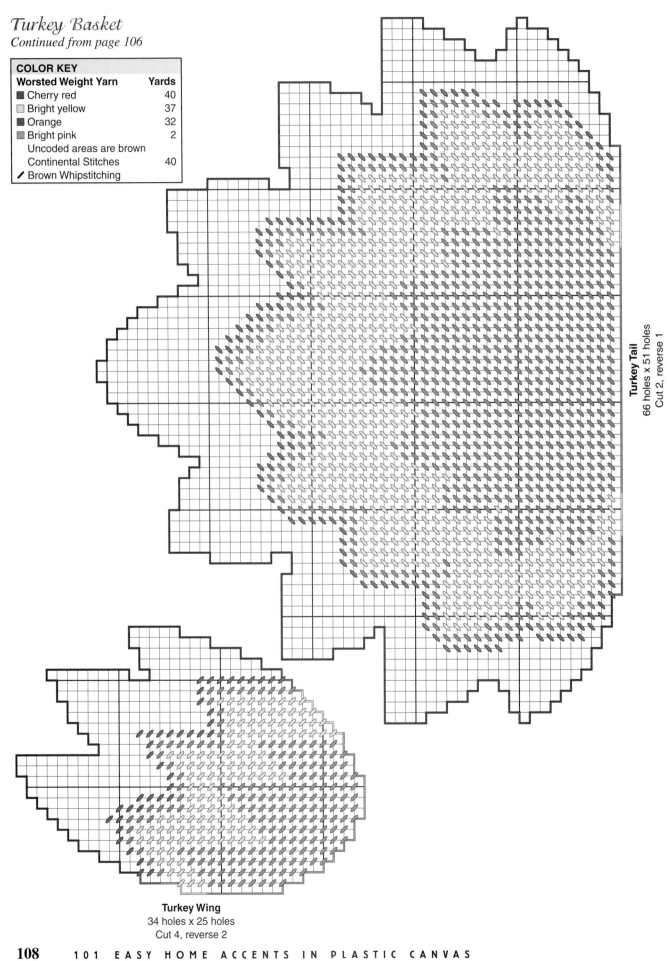

Turkey Tail
66 holes x 51 holes
Cut 2, reverse 1

Turkey Wing
34 holes x 25 holes
Cut 4, reverse 2

Gingerbread Candy House

Add this festive little house to your holiday decor.
Be sure to fill it with your grandkids' favorite treats!

Design by J. Sammi Johnson

TAKE NOTE

Skill Level: Beginner

Finished Size: 4¼ inches W x 4¾ inches H x 3¾ inches D

YOU'LL NEED

- ☐ 1 sheet brown 7-count plastic canvas
- ☐ 1 sheet clear 7-count plastic canvas
- ☐ Worsted weight yarn as listed in color key
- ☐ #16 tapestry needle
- ☐ 14 (6mm) green faceted beads
- ☐ 14 (6mm) red faceted beads
- ☐ Beading needle
- ☐ White sewing thread

INSTRUCTIONS

1 Cut gingerbread house front, back and sides from brown plastic canvas; cut roof pieces from clear plastic canvas according to graphs. Also cut one 22-hole x 22-hole piece for house bottom. House bottom will remain unstitched.

2 Stitch remaining pieces following graphs. With beading needle and white sewing thread, attach red and green beads to roof pieces where indicated on graph.

3 Using white through step 4, Whipstitch sides to front and back, then Whipstitch front, back and sides to unstitched bottom. Overcast top edges of house.

4 Whipstitch top edges of roof pieces together, Overcast remaining edges. Place roof on house and tack one roof piece to one side of house.

5 Thread a 5-inch length of white yarn from front to back through holes indicated with blue dots on the open side of the house. Tie yarn in a knot on inside of house, forming a ¾-inch loop. Secure loop over one of the center beads on roof. ∎

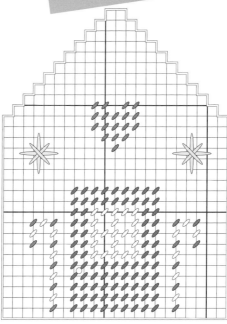

Gingerbread House Front & Back
22 holes x 29 holes
Cut 2 from brown

COLOR KEY	
Worsted Weight Yarn	**Yards**
☐ White	20
■ Green	3
■ Red	2
☐ Yellow	2
○ White French Knot	
● Attach green bead	
● Attach red bead	

Graphs continued on page 114

Christmas Cottage

Glistening snow on the roof of a quaint cottage makes this project both a lovely holiday decoration and an appealing gift!

Design by Angie Arickx

TAKE NOTE

Skill Level: Beginner

Finished Size: Approximately 6 inches W x 6 inches H x 3¾ inches D

YOU'LL NEED

- ☐ 1 sheet Darice Ultra Stiff 7-count plastic canvas
- ☐ Uniek Needloft plastic canvas yarn as listed in color key
- ☐ ⅛-inch-wide Plastic Canvas 7 metallic Needlepoint Yarn by Rainbow Gallery as listed in color key
- ☐ #16 tapestry needle

INSTRUCTIONS

1 Cut plastic canvas according to graphs. Cut one 29-hole x 21-hole piece for cottage bottom. Cottage bottom will remain unstitched.

2 Stitch remaining pieces following graphs. Work Backstitches and French Knots when background stitching is completed.

3 Using brown throughout,

Overcast top edges of cottage sides; Overcast roof edges of cottage front and back from dot to dot. Whipstitch front and back to sides, then Whipstitch front, back and sides to unstitched bottom.

4 Using white pearl through step 5, Whipstitch long straight edges of eaves to side edges on roof pieces between dots. Whipstitch wrong sides of roof pieces together along top edges. Overcast all remaining edges of roof and eaves except area between red dots on roof.

5 Overcast top edges of chimney sides, then Whipstitch together along side edges. Whipstitch bottom edges on opposite sides of chimney to roof between red dots. ∎

COLOR KEY	
Plastic Canvas Yarn	**Yards**
■ Red #01	15
□ Gold #17	11
■ Holly #27	12
□ Yellow # 57	7
✎ Brown #15 Backstitch, Overcasting and Whipstitching	15
✎ White #41 Backstitch	6
● Gold #17 French Knot	
⅛-Inch Metallic Needlepoint Yarn	
□ White pearl #PC10	25
Color numbers given are for Uniek Needloft plastic canvas yarn and Rainbow Gallery Plastic Canvas 7 Metallic Needlepoint Yarn.	

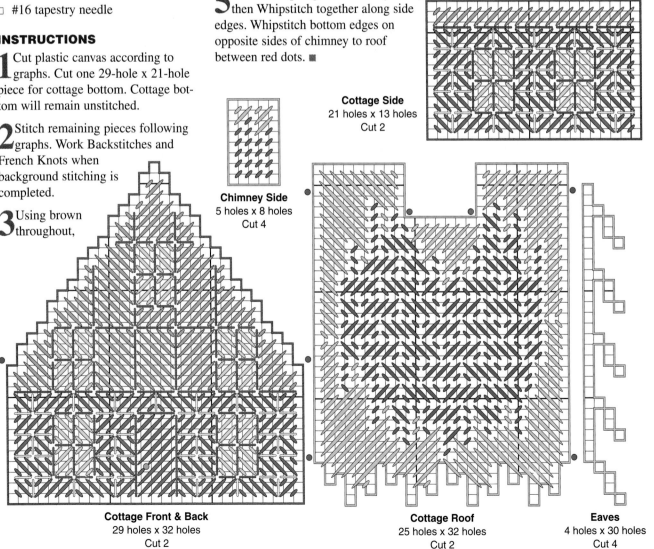

Chimney Side
5 holes x 8 holes
Cut 4

Cottage Side
21 holes x 13 holes
Cut 2

Cottage Front & Back
29 holes x 32 holes
Cut 2

Cottage Roof
25 holes x 32 holes
Cut 2

Eaves
4 holes x 30 holes
Cut 4

Holiday Gift Bag

Tuck a special Christmas gift inside this festive bag to give two-gifts-in-one!

Design by Mary T. Cosgrove

TAKE NOTE

Skill Level: Beginner

Finished Size: 5 inches W x 7½ inches H x 2¼ inches D

YOU'LL NEED

- ☐ 1 sheet Uniek Quick-Count 7-count plastic canvas
- ☐ Uniek Needloft plastic canvas yarn as listed in color key
- ☐ #16 tapestry needle

INSTRUCTIONS

1 Cut plastic canvas according to graphs. Cut two 9-hole x 9-hole pieces for bow sides.

2 Continental Stitch bow sides with Christmas red. Stitch remaining pieces following graphs, working uncoded areas on bag front and back with Christmas red Continental Stitches.

3 Using holly throughout, Overcast bag edges above bow on front and back; Overcast top edges of bag sides. Whipstitch bag bottom to front and back, then Whipstitch sides to bottom, front and back.

4 With Christmas red, Whipstitch bow sides to bows on front and back; Overcast remaining edges. ■

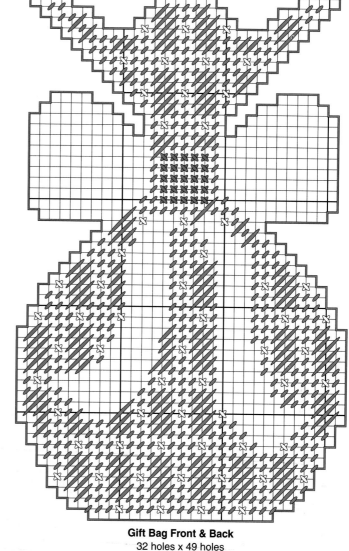

Gift Bag Front & Back
32 holes x 49 holes
Cut 2

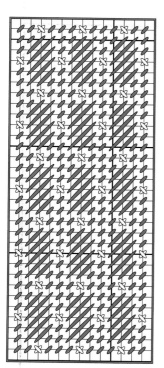

Gift Bag Side
14 holes x 32 holes
Cut 2

COLOR KEY	
Plastic Canvas Yarn	**Yards**
■ Christmas red #02	19
■ Holly #27	39
☐ White #41	12
Uncoded areas are Christmas red #02 Continental Stitches	19
Color numbers given are for Uniek Needloft plastic canvas yarn.	

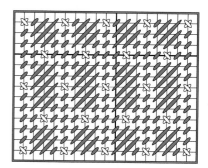

Gift Bag Bottom
18 holes x 14 holes
Cut 1

Gingerbread Candy House
Continued from page 109

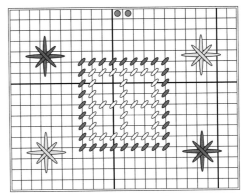

Gingerbread House Side
22 holes x 17 holes
Cut 2 from brown

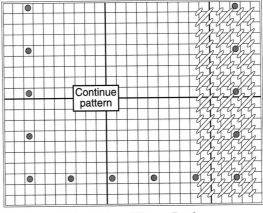

Continue
pattern

Gingerbread House Roof
25 holes x 19 holes
Cut 2 from clear

COLOR KEY	
Worsted Weight Yarn	**Yards**
☐ White	20
▪ Green	3
▪ Red	2
☐ Yellow	2
○ White French Knot	
● Attach green bead	
● Attach red bead	

Tips & Techniques

Many of us have computers and scanners in our homes. I was working on a gift box and liked the project so much, I knew I would make it again. I placed one completed side of the box on my scanner and made a color copy, then filed the page in my notebook of future project ideas. The copy clearly shows the colors and stitches used, and there's plenty of room on the page for adding any notes that would help me in the future.

—*Laura M. Meetze, South Carolina*

I tie a knot on the end of the yarn on the outside of the skein—*not* the inside yarn end, which feeds smoothly. This prevents me from using that end when I need several yards and it won't unwind very well from the outside of

the skein. When I see the knot, I know "knot" to use it.
—*Deb Arch, Illinois*

When you're not working on a project (or if you have just finished one), place it in a bag or tote with a fabric softener sheet. When you're ready to resume work on it, or when you want to give it to someone, your project will be clean—and it will smell nice, too.
—*Paula LaFramboise, Vermont*

When cutting plastic canvas, keep those little bits and pieces from falling on the floor or down between your cushions. Place a tray with sides, a large, flat gift box, or any large box with the sides cut down on your lap. Cut over it; the excess bits will fall in the box.
—*Helen Fedor, New Jersey*

I buy my yarn by the skein. I cut it into 18-inch lengths, then loosely knot together eight strands. I store each color in a clear plastic shoebox. For each new project, I put together my own "kit" of yarn colors.
—*Carole Ann Wilson, Massachusetts*

I use a black felt-tip marker to mark my plastic canvas for cutting. To remove the markings, a little nail-polish remover applied with a paper towel or napkin works like magic. The plastic canvas wipes clean instantly.
—*Vicky Oldenkamp, Iowa*

In place of more expensive raffia, I use ½-inch curling ribbon in my plastic canvas designs. For the 10- or 14-count plastic canvas, I use a ribbon shredder to shred it to fit. The price is great!
—*Synethia Nelson, New York*

Keepsake Decor

Combine your love of plastic canvas with your desire to create lasting, keepsake decorations for your home with this collection of creative and attractive projects!

Baby's First Christmas

Hang this special ornament from the mantel to celebrate your little one's very first Christmas!
Photo on page 115.

Design by Janelle Marie Giese

TAKE NOTE

Skill Level: Intermediate

Finished Size: 5¾ inches W x 6¼ inches H

YOU'LL NEED

- ☐ ½ sheet 7-count plastic canvas
- ☐ 2 small pieces 10-count plastic canvas
- ☐ Chenille yarn as listed in color key
- ☐ Kreinik ⅛-inch Ribbon as listed in color key
- ☐ Kreinik Fine (#8) Braid as listed in color key
- ☐ DMC #3 pearl cotton as listed in color key
- ☐ DMC #5 pearl cotton as listed in color key
- ☐ #16 tapestry needle

PROJECT NOTES

Work with 18-inch lengths of chenille yarn.

Many stitches do not cross corners of cut edges on graph; stitch exactly as shown so Overcast edge in opposite colors will be an even width.

INSTRUCTIONS

1 Cut teddy bear (page 126) from 7-count plastic canvas and stars from 10-count according to graphs.

2 Stitch teddy bear following graph. Overcast inside edges with off-white and outside edges with light tan and red following graph.

3 When background stitching is completed, Straight Stitch tongue with red ⅛-inch ribbon. Using black #5 pearl cotton throughout, work remaining Backstitches and Straight Stitches, stitching six times for each eye. Add French Knots to

teddy bear's muzzle.

4 Continental Stitch uncoded background on each star with very light old gold pearl cotton. When background stitching is completed, Straight Stitch arrows in points of each star with gold ⅛-inch ribbon.

5 Using mallard fine (#8) braid, Backstitch "Baby's First Christmas" on one star and baby's name and birth year on remaining star, referring to alphabet and numbers graph (page 126) and centering words in star.

6 For star hanger, knot one end of a length of black #5 pearl cotton and draw through top point of star, allowing tail to remain free.

7 Using gold ⅛-inch ribbon, Whipstitch wrong sides of stars together. Draw tail of pearl cotton into center back of teddy bear just above opening. Tie off, allowing a small gap to remain between teddy bear and star so star can turn freely.

8 For ornament hanger, thread a length of black #5 pearl cotton from front to back through holes indicated at top of teddy bear; knot ends, leaving a 3-inch loop. ∎

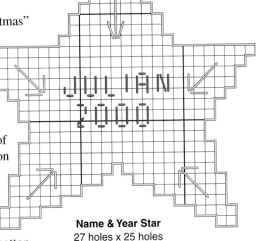

Name & Year Star
27 holes x 25 holes
Cut 1 from 10-count

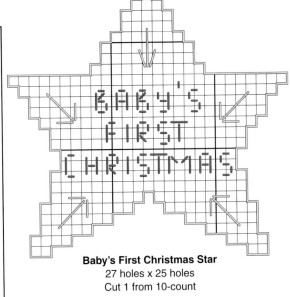

Baby's First Christmas Star
27 holes x 25 holes
Cut 1 from 10-count

COLOR KEY	
Chenille Yarn	**Yards**
☐ Off-white	7
■ Black	1
■ Light tan	9
⅛-Inch Ribbon	
■ Red #003	2
⟋ Gold #002 Straight Stitch and Whipstitching	3
⟋ Red #003 Straight Stitch	
Fine (#8) Braid	
⟋ Mallard #850 Backstitch	2
#3 Pearl Cotton	
Uncoded area is very light old gold #677 Continental Stitches	7
#5 Pearl Cotton	
⟋ Black #310 Backstitch and Straight Stitch	6
● Black #310 French Knot	
● Attach hanger	
Color numbers given are for Kreinik ⅛-inch Ribbon and Fine (#8) Braid, and DMC #3 and #5 pearl cotton.	

Graphs continued on page 126

Wee Ones Frames

Frame photos of your little sweethearts in this collection of seven delightful frames.

Designs by Nancy Marshall

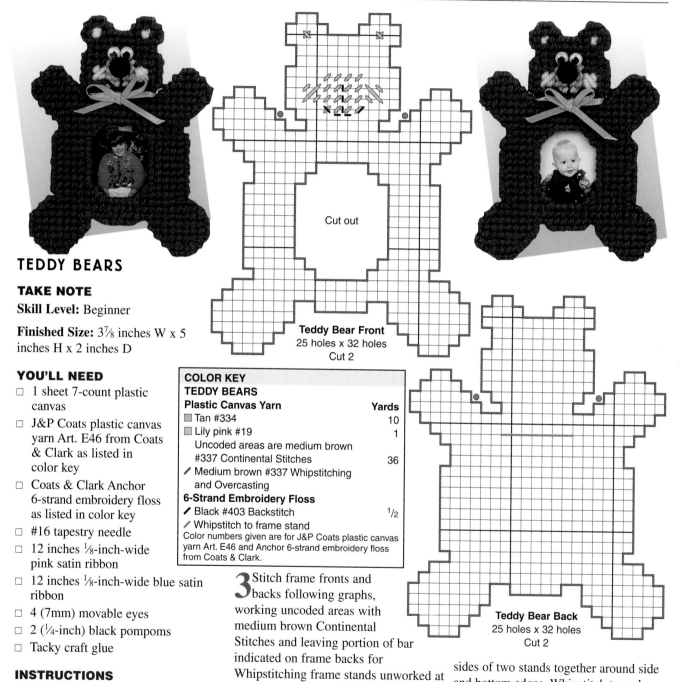

Teddy Bear Front
25 holes x 32 holes
Cut 2

Cut out

Teddy Bear Back
25 holes x 32 holes
Cut 2

TEDDY BEARS

TAKE NOTE

Skill Level: Beginner

Finished Size: 3⅞ inches W x 5 inches H x 2 inches D

YOU'LL NEED

- ☐ 1 sheet 7-count plastic canvas
- ☐ J&P Coats plastic canvas yarn Art. E46 from Coats & Clark as listed in color key
- ☐ Coats & Clark Anchor 6-strand embroidery floss as listed in color key
- ☐ #16 tapestry needle
- ☐ 12 inches ⅛-inch-wide pink satin ribbon
- ☐ 12 inches ⅛-inch-wide blue satin ribbon
- ☐ 4 (7mm) movable eyes
- ☐ 2 (¼-inch) black pompoms
- ☐ Tacky craft glue

COLOR KEY

TEDDY BEARS

Plastic Canvas Yarn	Yards
☐ Tan #334	10
☐ Lily pink #19	1
Uncoded areas are medium brown #337 Continental Stitches	36
✏ Medium brown #337 Whipstitching and Overcasting	

6-Strand Embroidery Floss

	Yards
✏ Black #403 Backstitch	½
✏ Whipstitch to frame stand	

Color numbers given are for J&P Coats plastic canvas yarn Art. E46 and Anchor 6-strand embroidery floss from Coats & Clark.

INSTRUCTIONS

1 Cut plastic canvas according to graphs. Cut four 7-hole x 19-hole pieces for frame stands.

2 Stitch frame stands with medium brown Continental Stitches.

3 Stitch frame fronts and backs following graphs, working uncoded areas with medium brown Continental Stitches and leaving portion of bar indicated on frame backs for Whipstitching frame stands unworked at this time.

4 Work black floss Backstitches on faces over completed background stitching.

5 Using medium brown through step 6, for each frame, Whipstitch wrong sides of two stands together around side and bottom edges. Whipstitch top edge to frame back where indicated on graph through all three thicknesses.

6 Overcast frame front and back around head and shoulder edges from dot to dot. Overcast frame opening.

Whipstitch wrong sides of front and back together along remaining edges.

7 Using photo as a guide, glue movable eyes and pompom to face front. Tie one length of ribbon in a bow around each neck; trim ends. Glue bows to secure.

ROCKET & STAR

TAKE NOTE

Skill Level: Beginner

Finished Size:

Rocket: 4 inches W x 5 inches H x 2 inches D

Star: 3½ inches W x 3¾ inches H x 1½ inches D

YOU'LL NEED

☐ 1 sheet 7-count plastic canvas
☐ J&P Coats plastic canvas yarn Art. E46 from Coats & Clark as listed in color key
☐ #16 tapestry needle
☐ Sequins: 5 each in red, green and blue
☐ Tacky craft glue

INSTRUCTIONS

1 Cut plastic canvas according to graphs. Cut two 7-hole x 20-hole pieces for rocket frame stand and two 7-hole x 15-hole pieces for star frame stand.

2 Stitch rocket frame stands with nickel Continental Stitches. Stitch star frame stands with honey gold Continental Stitches.

3 Stitch frame fronts and backs following graphs, working uncoded areas on rocket pieces with nickel Continental Stitches and leaving portion of bar indicated on frame backs for Whipstitching frame stands unworked at this time.

COLOR KEY	
ROCKET & STAR	
Plastic Canvas Yarn	**Yards**
☐ Honey gold #645	10
■ Olympic blue #849	3
■ Bright red #901	1
Uncoded areas are nickel #40 Continental Stitches	9
✎ Nickel #40 Overcasting and Whipstitching	
✎ Whipstitch to frame stand	
Color numbers given are for J&P Coats plastic canvas yarn Art. E46.	

4 Using honey gold for star and nickel for rocket, Whipstitch wrong sides of corresponding stand pieces together around side and bottom edges. Whipstitch top edges to corresponding frame backs where indicated on graphs through all three thicknesses.

5 Following graphs, Overcast around top edges of frame fronts and backs from dot to dot. Overcast frame openings. Whipstitch wrong sides of corresponding fronts and backs together along remaining edges.

6 Using photo as a guide, glue sequins to star.

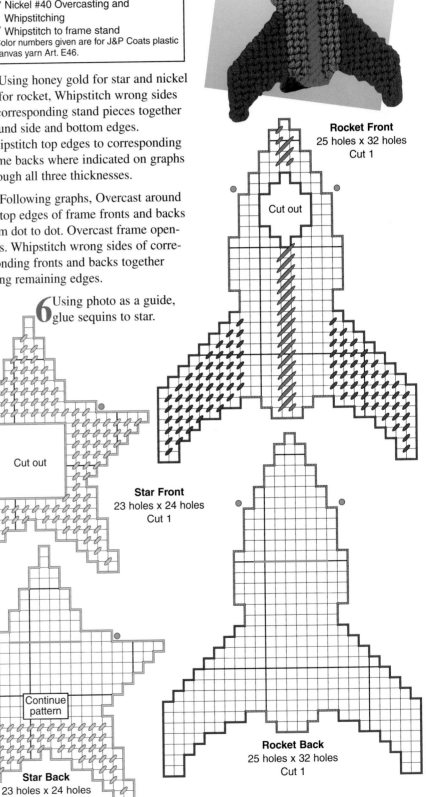

Rocket Front
25 holes x 32 holes
Cut 1

Cut out

Star Front
23 holes x 24 holes
Cut 1

Cut out

Star Back
23 holes x 24 holes
Cut 1

Continue pattern

Rocket Back
25 holes x 32 holes
Cut 1

CAR

TAKE NOTE

Skill Level: Beginner

Finished Size: 5 inches W x 3¾ inches H x 1⅜ inches D

YOU'LL NEED

- ☐ 1 sheet 7-count plastic canvas
- ☐ J&P Coats plastic canvas yarn Art. E46 from Coats & Clark as listed in color key
- ☐ #16 tapestry needle
- ☐ 14mm x 10mm crystal oval cabochon from The Beadery
- ☐ Tacky craft glue

INSTRUCTIONS

1 Cut plastic canvas according to graphs. Cut two 8-hole x 13-hole pieces for frame stand.

2 Stitch frame stand pieces with Olympic blue Continental Stitches.

3 Stitch frame fronts and backs following graphs, working uncoded areas on both pieces with Olympic blue Continental Stitches and leaving portion of bar indicated on frame back for Whipstitching frame stand unworked at this time.

4 With Olympic blue, Whipstitch wrong sides of stand pieces together around side and bottom edges. Whipstitch top edge to frame back where indicated on graph through all three thicknesses.

5 Following graphs, Overcast around top edges of frame front and back from dot to dot. Overcast frame opening. Whipstitch wrong sides of front and back together along remaining edges.

6 Using photo as a guide, glue cabochon to frame front for headlight.

COLOR KEY	
CAR	
Plastic Canvas Yarn	**Yards**
■ Black #12	3
▨ Nickel #401	2
■ Bright red #901	1
Uncoded areas are Olympic blue #849 Continental Stitches	13
⁄ Olympic blue #849 Overcasting and Whipstitching	
⁄ Whipstitch to frame stand	
Color numbers given are for J&P Coats plastic canvas yarn Art. E46.	

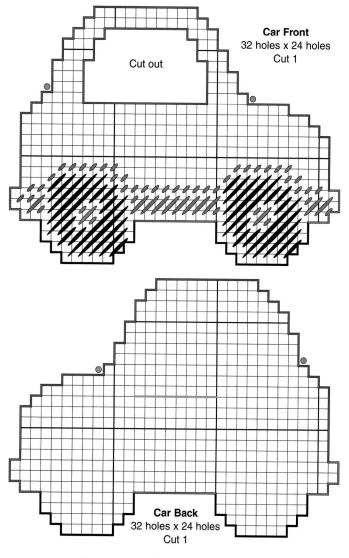

Cut out

Car Front
32 holes x 24 holes
Cut 1

Car Back
32 holes x 24 holes
Cut 1

EASTER EGG

TAKE NOTE

Skill Level: Beginner

Finished Size: 3¾ inches W x 4⅞ inches H x 12¼ inches D

YOU'LL NEED

☐ 1 sheet 7-count plastic canvas

☐ J&P Coats plastic canvas yarn Art. E46 from Coats & Clark as listed in color key

☐ #16 tapestry needle

INSTRUCTIONS

1 Cut plastic canvas according to graphs. Cut two 7-hole x 22-hole pieces for frame stand.

2 Stitch frame stand pieces with white Continental Stitches.

3 Stitch frame fronts and backs following graphs, working uncoded areas on both pieces with white Continental Stitches and leaving portion of bar indicated on frame back for Whipstitching frame stand unworked at this time.

4 With white, Whipstitch wrong sides of stand pieces together around side and bottom edges. Whipstitch top edge to frame back where indicated on graph through all three thicknesses.

5 Following graphs, Overcast around top edges of frame front and back from dot to dot. Overcast frame opening. Whipstitch wrong sides of front and back together along remaining edges.

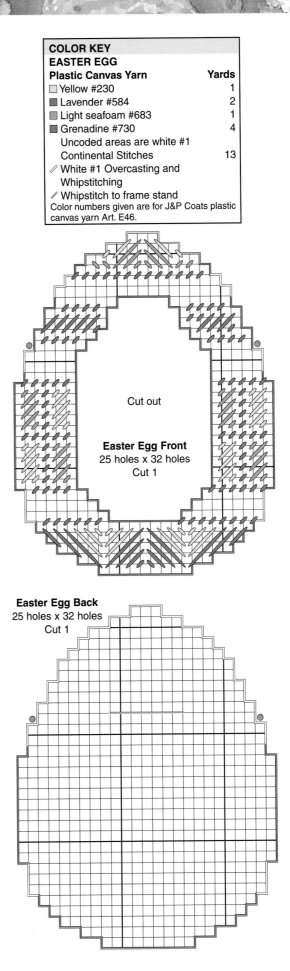

COLOR KEY	
EASTER EGG	
Plastic Canvas Yarn	**Yards**
☐ Yellow #230	1
▨ Lavender #584	2
▨ Light seafoam #683	1
▦ Grenadine #730	4
Uncoded areas are white #1	
Continental Stitches	13
⟋ White #1 Overcasting and Whipstitching	
⟋ Whipstitch to frame stand	
Color numbers given are for J&P Coats plastic canvas yarn Art. E46.	

Cut out

Easter Egg Front
25 holes x 32 holes
Cut 1

Easter Egg Back
25 holes x 32 holes
Cut 1

PUMPKIN

TAKE NOTE

Skill Level: Beginner

Finished Size: 5 inches W x 3⅞ inches H x 1½ inches D

YOU'LL NEED

- ☐ 1 sheet 7-count plastic canvas
- ☐ J&P Coats plastic canvas yarn Art. E46 from Coats & Clark as listed in color key
- ☐ #16 tapestry needle

INSTRUCTIONS

1 Cut plastic canvas according to graphs. Cut two 8-hole x 16-hole pieces for frame stand.

2 Stitch frame stand pieces with orange Continental Stitches.

3 Stitch frame fronts and backs following graphs, working uncoded areas on both pieces with orange Continental Stitches and leaving portion of bar indicated on frame back for Whipstitching frame stand unworked at this time.

4 When background stitching is completed, work tangerine Backstitches on pumpkin front.

5 With orange, Whipstitch wrong sides of stand pieces together around side and bottom edges. Whipstitch top edge to frame back where indicated on graph through all three thicknesses.

6 Following graphs, Overcast around top edges of frame front and back from dot to dot. Overcast frame opening. Whipstitch wrong sides of front and back together along remaining edges. ∎

COLOR KEY		
PUMPKIN		
Plastic Canvas Yarn		**Yards**
■ Medium brown #337		1
■ Tangerine #253		4
Uncoded areas are orange #245 Continental Stitches		15
⁄ Tangerine #253 Backstitch		
⁄ Orange #245 Overcasting		
⁄ Whipstitch to frame stand		
Color numbers given are for J&P Coats plastic canvas yarn Art. E46.		

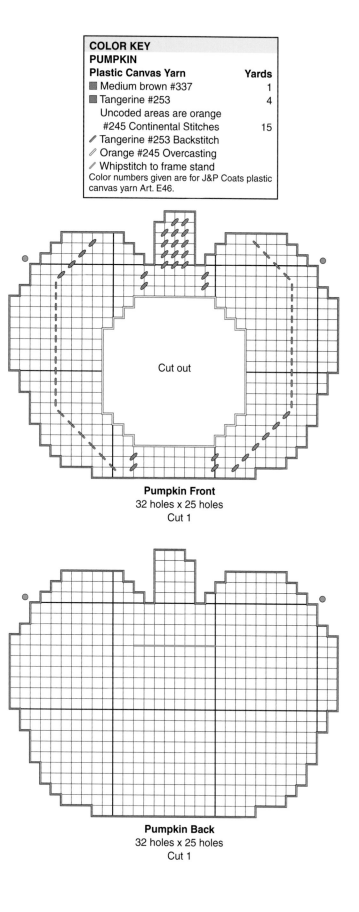

Pumpkin Front
32 holes x 25 holes
Cut 1

Cut out

Pumpkin Back
32 holes x 25 holes
Cut 1

Elegant Music Box

Stitched with beautiful chenille yarn, this lovely project is both a keepsake box and music box!

Design by Janelle Marie Giese

TAKE NOTE

Skill Level: Advanced

Finished Size: 5 inches W x 6 inches H x 5 inches D

YOU'LL NEED

☐ 1½ sheets black 7-count plastic canvas
☐ Lion Brand Chenille Sensations yarn as listed in color key
☐ Kreinik ⅛-inch Ribbon as listed in color key
☐ #16 tapestry needle
☐ Key wind musical movement
☐ 4 (⅜-inch x 1⅜-inch) mini shaker pegs
☐ Black acrylic paint
☐ Varnish or sealer (optional)
☐ Paintbrush
☐ 18 inches (2-inch-wide) black fringe with flat top
☐ 18 inches black braided trim
☐ 1½-inch silk flower in coordinating color
☐ Straight pins
☐ Thick white glue

PROJECT NOTE

Work with 18-inch lengths of chenille yarn.

CUTTING & STITCHING

1 Cut plastic canvas according to graphs. Cut four 29-hole x 6-hole pieces for box corners, four 24-hole x 4-hole pieces for lid sides and four 6-hole x 4-hole pieces for lid side corners.

2 Also cut the following which will remain unstitched: two 14-hole x 9-hole and two 17-hole x 9-hole pieces for music box casing and four 5-hole x 9-hole and four 21-hole x 9-hole pieces for interior floor sides.

3 Following graph and matching edges, place the two box base pieces together and Continental Stitch as one with black through both thicknesses, leaving bars with green lines unstitched. Work stitches in corners of leg openings as indicated. Overcast key opening, but do not Overcast leg openings.

4 For music box casing, using black, Whipstitch short sides to long sides, then Whipstitch sides to wrong side of base where indicated with green lines.

5 Following graphs, stitch box sides and lid, working antique gold stitches first. Work uncoded areas with black Continental Stitches.

COLOR KEY	
Chenille Yarn	**Yards**
■ Black #153	89
■ London print #401	13
Uncoded areas are black #153 Continental Stitches	
⅛-Inch Ribbon	
☐ Antique gold #205C	12
╱ Attach fringe	
Color numbers given are for Lion Brand Chenille Sensations yarn and Kreinik ⅛-inch Ribbon.	

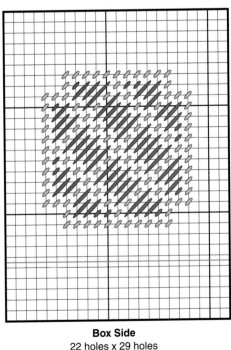

Box Side
22 holes x 29 holes
Cut 4

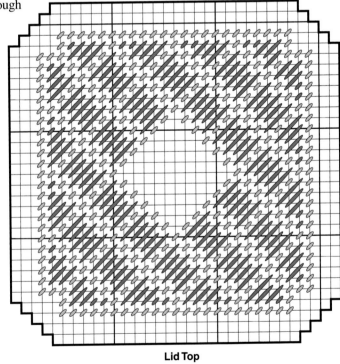

Lid Top
32 holes x 32 holes
Cut 1

6 Using black through step 8, Continental Stitch box corners. Whipstitch corners to box sides, then Whipstitch sides to base; Overcast top edges.

7 Continental Stitch lid sides and lid side corners. Whipstitch 4-hole edges of lid sides to lid side corners, then Whipstitch to lid top; Overcast bottom edges.

8 Continental Stitch interior floor. Whip-stitch 9-hole edges of interior floor sides together, alternating the 5-hole and 21-hole lengths, then Whipstitch top edges of floor sides to floor, forming a table.

FINAL ASSEMBLY

1 For legs, paint shaker pegs with black acrylic paint; allow to dry. If desired, apply varnish or sealer; allow to dry.

2 Glue legs into leg openings of base. Place music box into casing, aligning key hole. Push key through opening in base and twist into music box. Slide foundation into box over music box casing.

3 Glue fringe around lower edge of box, aligning top edge of fringe with fringe line indicated on box sides. Push straight pins through fringe into box to hold until dry.

4 Glue braid over top edge of fringe, securing with straight pins until dry.

5 Glue flower to center top of lid. ■

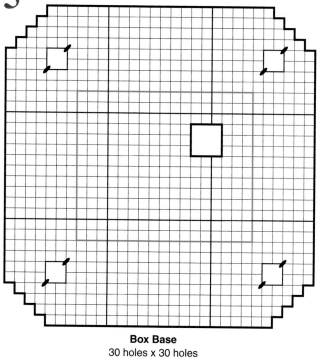

Box Base
30 holes x 30 holes
Cut 2

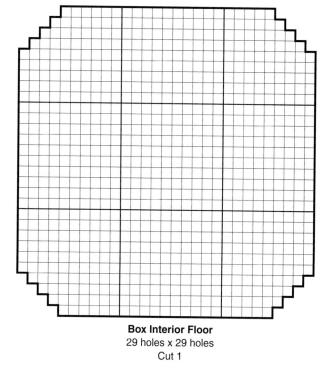

Box Interior Floor
29 holes x 29 holes
Cut 1

Family Photo Box

*Keep your collection of family photographs close at hand
in this colorful box for sharing with visitors.*

Design by Joan Green

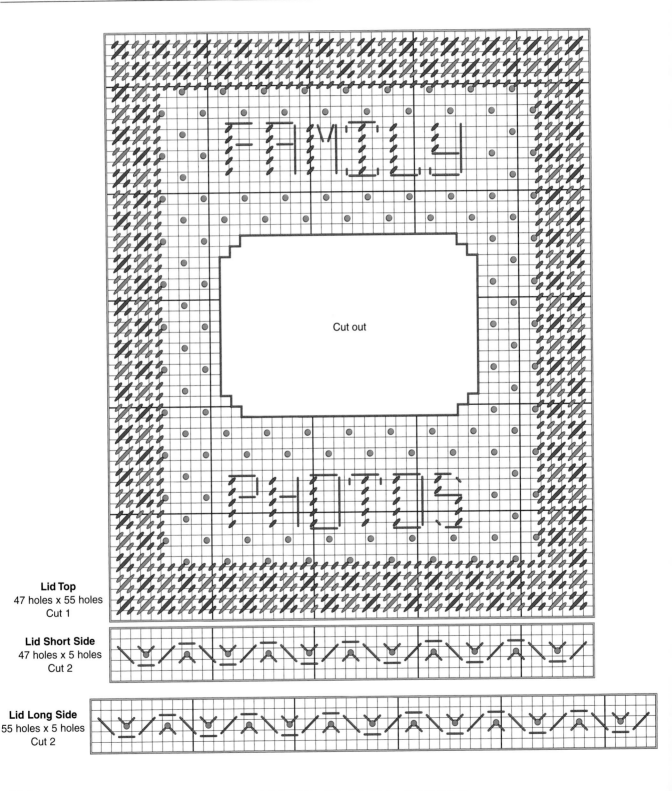

Lid Top
47 holes x 55 holes
Cut 1

Lid Short Side
47 holes x 5 holes
Cut 2

Lid Long Side
55 holes x 5 holes
Cut 2

Cut out

TAKE NOTE

Skill Level: Beginner

Finished Size: 7¼ inches W x 8½ inches L x 5¾ inches D

YOU'LL NEED

- ☐ 2 sheets Darice Ultra Stiff 7-count plastic canvas
- ☐ Spinrite Bernat Berella "4" worsted weight yarn as listed in color key
- ☐ #16 tapestry needle
- ☐ Lightweight cardboard
- ☐ Sheet cashmere tan self-adhesive Presto felt from Kunin Felt
- ☐ Colored poster board (optional)
- ☐ Fabric glue

INSTRUCTIONS

1 Cut plastic canvas according to graphs (pages 124 and 126). Cut one 46-hole x 54-hole piece for box bottom. Box bottom will remain unstitched.

2 Stitch pieces following graphs, working uncoded areas with light tapestry gold Continental Stitches.

3 When background stitching is completed, work Straight Stitches on lid top and sides with four plies yarn. Work strawberry passion French Knots on lid top with 2 plies yarn; work strawberry passion French Knots on lid sides with 4 plies yarn.

4 Using light tapestry gold through step 5, Whipstitch box long sides to box short sides, then Whipstitch sides to box bottom. Overcast top edges.

COLOR KEY	
Worsted Weight Yarn	**Yards**
■ Strawberry passion #8706	40
■ Pretty purple #8708	40
■ Medium ocean #8762	24
☐ Light tapestry gold #8886	70
Uncoded areas are light tapestry gold #8886 Continental Stitches	
╱ Pretty purple #8708 Straight Stitch	
╱ Medium ocean #8762 Straight Stitch	
● Strawberry passion #8706 4-ply French Knot	
● Strawberry passion #8706 2-ply French Knot	
Color numbers given are for Spinrite Bernat Berella "4" worsted weight yarn.	

5 Whipstitch lid long sides to lid short sides, then Whipstitch sides to lid top. Overcast bottom edges. Overcast opening on lid top with purple passion.

6 Cut felt to fit box bottom, then attach to bottom of box.

7 Cut cardboard to line box sides and lid top. Glue photo to cardboard lid liner so photo shows through lid

opening. Lightly glue cardboard to wrong side of lid top and box sides.

8 Optional: Cut index-style dividers from colored poster board to fit inside box to separate photos. ■

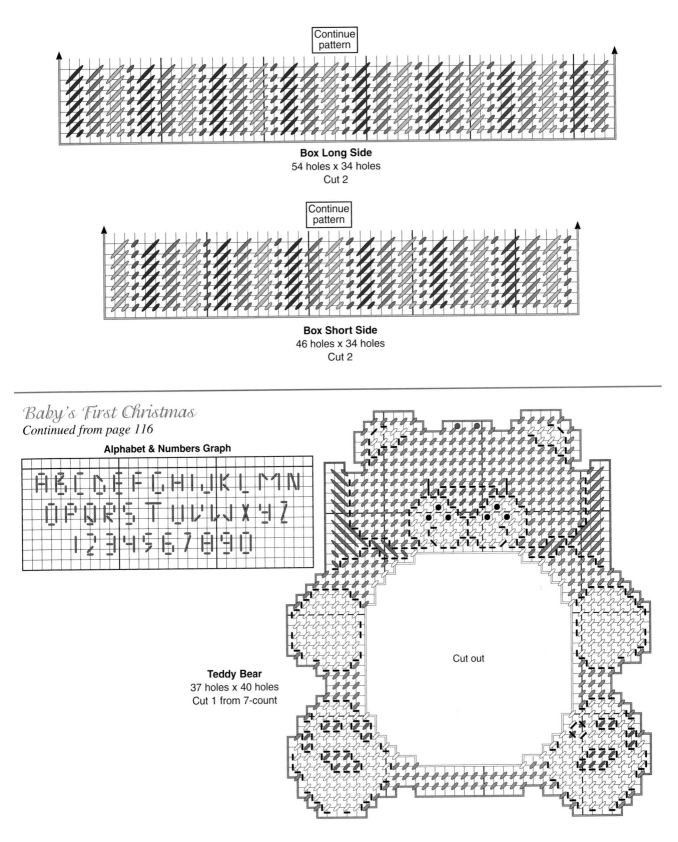

Continue pattern

Box Long Side
54 holes x 34 holes
Cut 2

Continue pattern

Box Short Side
46 holes x 34 holes
Cut 2

Baby's First Christmas
Continued from page 116

Alphabet & Numbers Graph

Teddy Bear
37 holes x 40 holes
Cut 1 from 7-count

Cut out

Dreamland Angel

Help your youngster overcome nighttime anxieties by giving her this charming keepsake angel to be with her as she sleeps!

Design by Lee Lindeman

TAKE NOTE

Skill Level: Intermediate

Finished Size: 8 inches W x 11½ inches H x 5⅞ inches D

YOU'LL NEED

- ☐ 2 sheets 7-count plastic canvas
- ☐ Worsted weight yarn as listed in color key
- ☐ #16 tapestry needle
- ☐ 3 (¼-inch) pink buttons
- ☐ 2 (3mm) black round beads
- ☐ Sewing needle and pale pink sewing thread
- ☐ 2 (⅞-inch) star buttons
- ☐ Sheet white craft foam
- ☐ Natural jute mini curl doll hair
- ☐ 1½ yards ¾-inch wide white lace
- ☐ 1 yard glitter cord
- ☐ Polyester fiberfill
- ☐ 7 inches ⅛-inch dowel
- ☐ White acrylic paint
- ☐ Paintbrush
- ☐ Dental floss
- ☐ 4½-inch in diameter wooden disk
- ☐ White plush felt
- ☐ Hand drill
- ☐ ⅛-inch drill bit
- ☐ Hot-glue gun

CUTTING & STITCHING

1 Cut plastic canvas according to graphs.

2 Using pattern given, cut wings from white craft foam. Set aside.

3 Stitch pieces following graphs, reversing two sleeves, two feet and two hands before stitching. Work entire head back with light pink Continental Stitches.

4 With sewing needle and pale pink sewing thread attach black beads to head front where indicated on graph; attach buttons to robe front where indicated on graph.

5 Using light pink through step 6, Whipstitch wrong sides of head pieces together, leaving bottom edges unstitched. Stuff lightly with fiberfill.

6 Matching edges, Whipstitch wrong sides of two hand pieces together. Repeat with remaining hands. Matching edges, Whipstitch wrong sides of two foot pieces together. Repeat with remaining foot pieces.

7 Using white through step 8, Whipstitch wrong sides of robe pieces together along side edges. Overcast neck and hem edges. Stuff with a small amount of fiberfill.

8 Matching edges, Whipstitch two sleeve pieces together along side and top edges. Overcast bottom edges. Stuff with a small amount of fiberfill. Repeat with remaining sleeve pieces.

ASSEMBLY

1 Paint dowel with white acrylic paint. Allow to dry. Set aside.

2 Using photo as a guide throughout assembly, glue jute hair around edge of head, placing two longer pieces of hair at the top. Pull longer pieces down over forehead and glue in place. Glue one star button to hair on forehead.

3 Glue lace inside each sleeve and inside robe around bottom edges. Glue one hand inside each sleeve where indicated on graph between blue dots. Glue feet inside hem area of robe.

4 Glue neck of head into neck of robe. Gather an 8-inch length of lace with dental floss and glue around neck.

5 Glue glitter cord around edges of wings, then glue wings to back of angel.

6 Drill a ⅛-inch hole in center top of wooden disk. Cover disk with felt, then cut a hole in felt over drilled hole. Glue felt in place. Glue glitter cord around edge of disk.

7 Glue one end of dowel into hole in disk; glue other end inside robe between feet.

8 Glue remaining star button to felt on disk. ∎

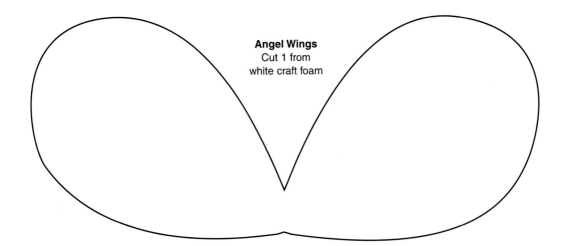

Angel Wings
Cut 1 from
white craft foam

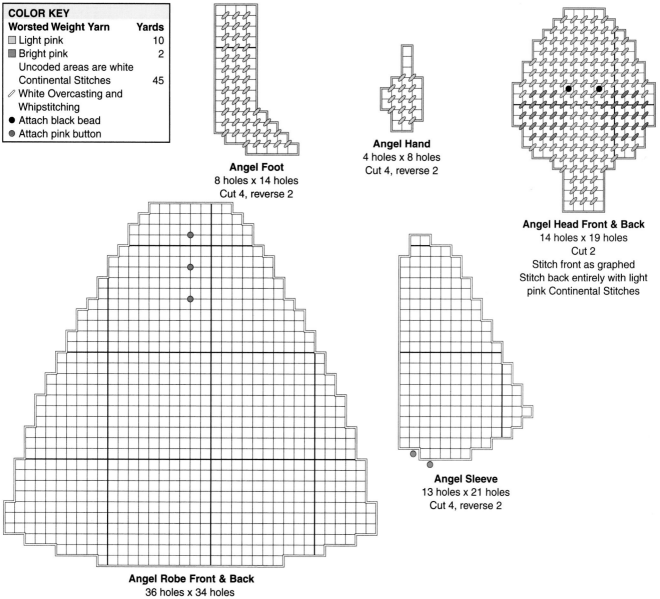

COLOR KEY

Worsted Weight Yarn	Yards
☐ Light pink	10
◼ Bright pink	2
Uncoded areas are white Continental Stitches	45
⁄ White Overcasting and Whipstitching	
● Attach black bead	
● Attach pink button	

Angel Foot
8 holes x 14 holes
Cut 4, reverse 2

Angel Hand
4 holes x 8 holes
Cut 4, reverse 2

Angel Head Front & Back
14 holes x 19 holes
Cut 2
Stitch front as graphed
Stitch back entirely with light
pink Continental Stitches

Angel Sleeve
13 holes x 21 holes
Cut 4, reverse 2

Angel Robe Front & Back
36 holes x 34 holes
Cut 2

Tips & Techniques

Don't throw away your scrap plastic canvas! I bought a 2-foot Christmas tree that I keep up all year round. I use my scrap plastic canvas to make ornaments for the upcoming holiday. For example, for the Fourth of July, I make stars, flags and firecrackers and hang them on my tree with mini white lights. I display my tree year-round in my living room window.
—*Doris Coffey, Ohio*

I have barrels and barrels full of yarn, so I find it difficult to keep track of the different colors. So, I decided to type the colors and amounts of each ionto my computer.

Now if a project calls for a certain color of yarn, all I do is slide in a disk, open a file and see what colors I have. It is much faster than searching through my closet for the right color. If you have a computer, you can use this nifty time-saving tip too!
—*Heather Monroe, Nevada*

I keep my yarn and instruction books, needles and scissors in a school back pack I bought at a thrift store for $1. It's the best buck I ever spent!

This pack has small pockets on the outside that everything fits into perfectly. I have another pack in which I keep my current project plus supplies. Whenever I'm headed out and know

I'll have to wait (i.e. doctor's office or waiting for kids), I just grab my pack and go. I can get a lot done in those few minutes of waiting!
—*Lisa Fleming, Iowa*

I don't like to cut plastic canvas on my carpet because all the little nubs get worked down into the carpet and are difficult to remove. While planning to stitch at my sister's house, and not wanting to get nubs in her carpet, I took the plastic bag wrap the project kit came in and slipped it over my hands. I then cut the canvas inside the bag. The little nubs fell into the bag, not all over the carpet. I could easily see where I was cutting through the plastic bag.
—*Jennie Robinson, Florida*

Teddy Bear Love Frame

*Guests in your home will ooh and ahh when they see
your little darling framed in this delightful project!*

Design by Angie Arickx

TAKE NOTE

Skill Level: Beginner

Finished Size: $12\frac{3}{8}$ inches W x 14
inches H x $3\frac{5}{8}$ inches D

YOU'LL NEED

- ☐ 1 artist-size sheet Darice Ultra Stiff
  7-count plastic canvas
- ☐ Uniek Needloft plastic canvas yarn
  as listed in color key
- ☐ #16 tapestry needle

- ☐ 8-inch x 10-inch piece double-sided
  adhesive
- ☐ 8-inch x 10-inch vertical acrylic
  frame with stand

INSTRUCTIONS

1 Cut plastic canvas according to graph.

2 Stitch and Overcast piece following
graph, working uncoded areas with
lavender Continental Stitches.

3 Using double-sided adhesive, attach
stitched teddy bear frame to front of
acrylic frame, making sure to cut out
photo opening from double-sided adhesive
before attaching to acrylic frame front. ∎

Teddy Bear Love Frame
82 holes x 95 holes
Cut 1

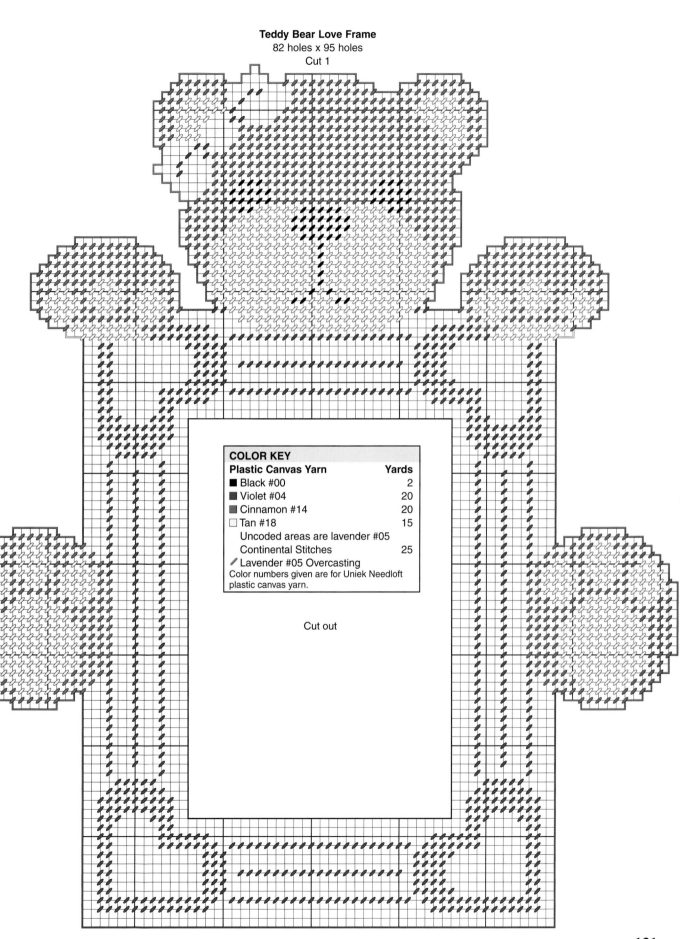

COLOR KEY

Plastic Canvas Yarn	Yards
■ Black #00	2
■ Violet #04	20
■ Cinnamon #14	20
□ Tan #18	15
Uncoded areas are lavender #05 Continental Stitches	25
╱ Lavender #05 Overcasting	

Color numbers given are for Uniek Needloft plastic canvas yarn.

Cut out

Quilt-Style Photo Cube

Show off your favorite family photographs in this attractive photo cube! Work it in colors to match your decor.

Design by Angie Arickx

TAKE NOTE

Skill Level: Beginner

Finished Size: 5¾ inches W x 5¾ inches H x 5¾ inches D

YOU'LL NEED

☐ 2 sheets Darice Ultra Stiff 7-count plastic canvas

☐ Uniek Needloft plastic canvas yarn as listed in color key

☐ #16 tapestry needle

PROJECT NOTE

Photo openings are 3 inches square.

INSTRUCTIONS

1 Cut plastic canvas according to graphs. Cut one 35-hole x 35-hole piece for inner cube bottom. Cut four 35-hole x 36-hole pieces for inner cube sides. All inner cube pieces will remain unstitched.

2 Stitch outer cube pieces following graphs, working uncoded areas with black Continental Stitches.

3 Using sail blue throughout, Overcast inside and bottom edges of outer cube sides. Whipstitch outer cube sides together, then Whipstitch sides to top. Whipstitch inner cube sides together, then Whipstitch sides to inner cube bottom.

4 Slide outer cube over inner cube, securing photos as desired. ∎

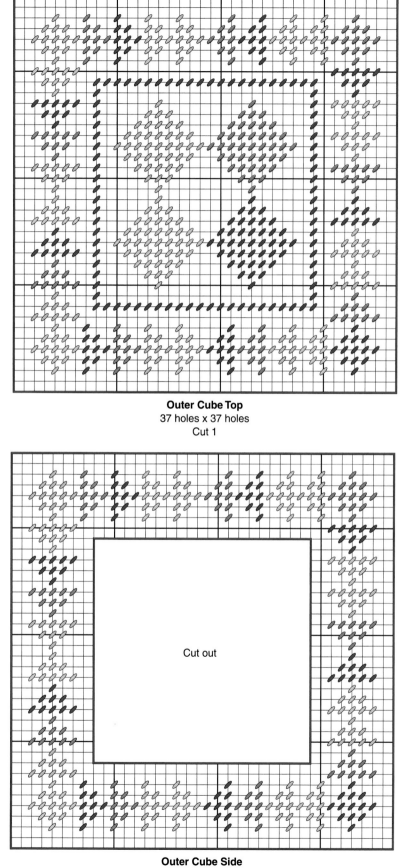

Outer Cube Top
37 holes x 37 holes
Cut 1

Outer Cube Side
37 holes x 37 holes
Cut 4

Cut out

COLOR KEY	
Plastic Canvas Yarn	**Yards**
☐ Lavender #05	11
☐ Pink #07	11
■ Sail blue #35	30
☐ Baby blue #36	11
Uncoded areas are black #00	
Continental Stitches	46
Color numbers given are for Uneik Needloft plastic canvas yarn.	

Tips & Techniques

I covered a small box, about 14" square, with pretty adhesive-backed paper. I label this box with my granddaughter's name, and in it I put all my sewing and crafting leftovers—small pieces of plastic canvas, lace, ribbon, small balls of yarn, etc. I'll keep adding to this box for about a year, then add a few wooden shapes, clothespins and doll stands, and mail it to her. This "Pandora's Box" will encourage her to become a crafter.
—*Wilma Shay, Texas*

Some stacking crates have inside lips that fit file folders perfectly. I use several of these to hold plastic canvas magazines, pattern leaflets and old calendars and stack them out of the way. This is less expensive than a filing cabinet and is also portable when the need arises.
—*Beverly Riddle, Indiana*

When making Turkey Loops, I stitch the yarn around a plastic straw or something smaller so all my loops come out the same size.
—*Mavis Johnson, North Carolina*

Many projects require that identical pieces of plastic canvas be cut (for another side, backing, etc.). So that I don't have to count and recount to cut the second piece, I use the worked piece as a pattern. I lay it on the blank plastic canvas, then secure the pieces together with several metal paper clips, or a few long basting stitches through both layers. This keeps the pieces from slipping as I cut. This also is a great way to hold pieces in place while you're Whipstitching them together.
—*Dottie Ann Linville, Ohio*

Chapter Seven

Table-Top Treasures

*This collection of accents for table tops is just what
you need for adding a finished festive touch to your dinner
or party table, or for adding something special to
end tables and shelves throughout your home.*

Polly Pumpkin & Callie Cat Centerpieces

Who can resist these whimsical centerpieces? They're sure to add laughter and life to your Halloween party!

Designs by Lee Lindeman

POLLY PUMPKIN

TAKE NOTE

Skill Level: Intermediate

Finished Size: 7¼ inches W x 10½ inches H x 6¾ inches D

YOU'LL NEED

- ☐ 2 sheets 7-count plastic canvas
- ☐ Coats & Clark Red Heart Super Saver worsted weight yarn Art. E301 as listed in color key
- ☐ 6-strand embroidery floss as listed in color key
- ☐ #16 tapestry needle
- ☐ Natural jute curly doll hair
- ☐ Polyester fiberfill
- ☐ 4¾-inch terra-cotta pot
- ☐ 6-inch Styrofoam plastic foam disc from Dow Chemical Company
- ☐ Craft stick
- ☐ 20 inches 1½-inch-wide green ribbon
- ☐ 2½ inches ½-inch in diameter tree branch
- ☐ Natural excelsior
- ☐ 11-inch square burlap
- ☐ Natural raffia
- ☐ Hot-glue gun

INSTRUCTIONS

1 Cut plastic canvas according to graphs (page 137), cutting out holes on pumpkin front only, leaving pumpkin back intact.

2 Stitch pieces following graphs, working uncoded areas on front with orange Continental Stitches. Stitch back entirely with orange Continental Stitches.

3 Overcast inside edges of front with orange and white, following graph.

Work Backstitches, Straight Stitch and French Knots with embroidery floss when background stitching and Overcasting are completed.

4 Using photo as a guide through step 7, place eyes behind openings on front with white stitches to the left; glue in place. Place mouth behind opening on front; glue in place.

5 Overcast nose with black. And glue to pumpkin front.

6 Using orange throughout, on pumpkin front and back, Overcast top edges from dot to dot and bottom edges from dot to dot. Whipstitch wrong sides together along remaining edges.

7 Glue tree branch in top opening for stem. Stuff pumpkin with fiberfill. Glue craft stick half way into bottom of pumpkin.

FINAL ASSEMBLY

1 Cut plastic foam disc to fit inside top of terra-cotta pot just below rim. Glue excess plastic foam pieces into bottom of pot, then glue cut disc in place.

2 Insert bottom half of craft stick into center of plastic foam disc. Remove stick and put glue in slit made, then insert craft stick back into slit.

3 Using photo as a guide through step 5, glue excelsior around top of plastic foam and bottom of pumpkin.

4 Glue jute curly hair to top of pumpkin. Tie ribbon in a bow around stem at top of pumpkin.

5 Fringe edges of burlap. Place pot in center of burlap, then wrap up around pot; glue in place. Tie a few strands of raffia in a bow around burlap-covered pot.

CALLIE CAT

TAKE NOTE

Skill Level: Intermediate

Finished Size: 6⅞ inches W x 6 inches H x 2¼ inches D

YOU'LL NEED

- ☐ 1 sheet 7-count plastic canvas
- ☐ Coats & Clark Red Heart Super Saver worsted weight yarn Art. E301 as listed in color key
- ☐ 6-strand embroidery floss as listed in color key
- ☐ #16 tapestry needle
- ☐ Small amount polyester fiberfill
- ☐ 3 (⅝-inch) red heart buttons
- ☐ 8mm brown animal eyes
- ☐ 9mm black cabochon
- ☐ 10 inches ¼-inch-wide yellow satin ribbon
- ☐ Hot-glue gun

INSTRUCTIONS

1 Cut plastic canvas according to graphs (pages 137 and 138).

2 Stitch pieces following graphs, working uncoded areas with black Continental Stitches. Stitch head back and body back entirely with black Continental Stitches.

3 When background stitching is completed, work black embroidery floss Straight Stitch on cat face.

4 With black, Overcast bottom edges of body front and back; Overcast top edges from dot to dot. Whipstitch wrong sides of front and back together along remaining edges. Stuff with fiberfill.

5 Whipstitch wrong sides of feet together with black and white following graph. Glue feet to bottom of assembled body, enclosing stuffing in body.

6 Whipstitch head front and back together with black, stuffing with fiberfill before closing. Using photo as a guide through step 9, glue eyes to head; glue cabochon to head for nose. Glue neck of head into neck of body.

7 Matching edges, Whipstitch one arm front to one arm back following

graph. Repeat with remaining arm pieces. Glue arms to body back at shoulders.

8 Whipstitch wrong sides of tail pieces together with black. Glue to body back.

9 Glue heart buttons to white part of body front. Tie ribbon in a bow around cat's neck. ▣

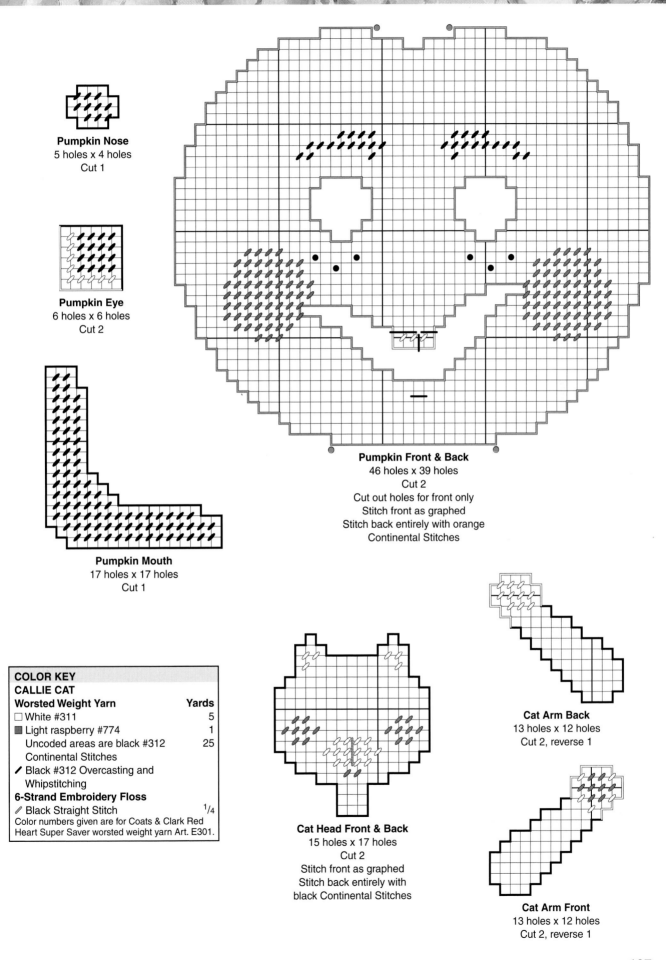

Pumpkin Nose
5 holes x 4 holes
Cut 1

Pumpkin Eye
6 holes x 6 holes
Cut 2

Pumpkin Mouth
17 holes x 17 holes
Cut 1

Pumpkin Front & Back
46 holes x 39 holes
Cut 2
Cut out holes for front only
Stitch front as graphed
Stitch back entirely with orange
Continental Stitches

COLOR KEY
CALLIE CAT

Worsted Weight Yarn	Yards
☐ White #311	5
◼ Light raspberry #774	1
Uncoded areas are black #312	25
Continental Stitches	
✎ Black #312 Overcasting and Whipstitching	

6-Strand Embroidery Floss
| ✎ Black Straight Stitch | 1/4 |

Color numbers given are for Coats & Clark Red Heart Super Saver worsted weight yarn Art. E301.

Cat Head Front & Back
15 holes x 17 holes
Cut 2
Stitch front as graphed
Stitch back entirely with
black Continental Stitches

Cat Arm Back
13 holes x 12 holes
Cut 2, reverse 1

Cat Arm Front
13 holes x 12 holes
Cut 2, reverse 1

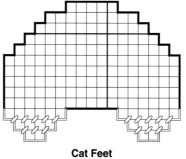

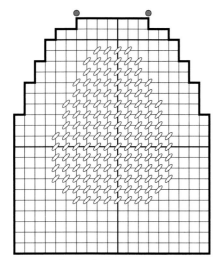

Cat Body Front & Back
19 holes x 22 holes
Cut 2
Stitch front as graphed
Stitch back entirely with
black Continental Stitches

Cat Feet
17 holes x 13 holes
Cut 2

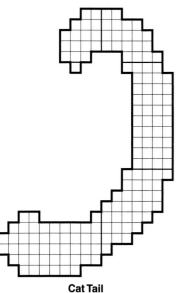

Cat Tail
17 holes x 25 holes
Cut 2, reverse 1

COLOR KEY
CALLIE CAT

Worsted Weight Yarn	Yards
☐ White #311	5
■ Light raspberry #774	1
Uncoded areas are black #312 Continental Stitches	25

✦ Black #312 Overcasting and
Whipstitching

6-Strand Embroidery Floss
🖊 Black Straight Stitch   ¼
Color numbers given are for Coats & Clark Red
Heart Super Saver worsted weight yarn Art. E301.

Harvest Favor Cart

Filled with nuts or candies this small project makes a delightful table favor!

Design by Mary T. Cosgrove

TAKE NOTE

Skill Level: Intermediate

Finished Size: 1⅞ inches W x 4 inches L x 1⅞ inches H

YOU'LL NEED

- ☐ ½ sheet Uniek Quick-Count 7-count plastic canvas
- ☐ 2 (3-inch) plastic canvas radial circles by Darice
- ☐ Uniek Needloft plastic canvas yarn as listed in color key
- ☐ #16 tapestry needle
- ☐ Hot-glue gun

CUTTING & STITCHING

1 Cut plastic canvas according to graphs, cutting away gray area on wheels.

2 Stitch pieces following graphs, reversing one side and one handle before stitching. Do not stitch bar with blue line on cart side.

3 Using cinnamon through step 4, Overcast wheels. Matching edges and with wrong sides facing, Whipstitch handles to handles on cart, leaving handle edges adjacent to cart unstitched at this time.

4 Whipstitch cart front and back to cart sides, Whipstitching adjacent handle edges to cart back and sides at blue line on side through all three thicknesses. Whipstitch bottom to front, back and sides; Overcast top edges of assembled cart.

5 Using photo as a guide, glue wheels to cart. ▪

COLOR KEY	
Plastic Canvas Yarn	**Yards**
■ Cinnamon #14	6
▨ Sandstone #16	5
☐ Camel #43	3
✎ Cinnamon #14 Backstitch	
Color numbers given are for Uniek Needloft plastic canvas yarn.	

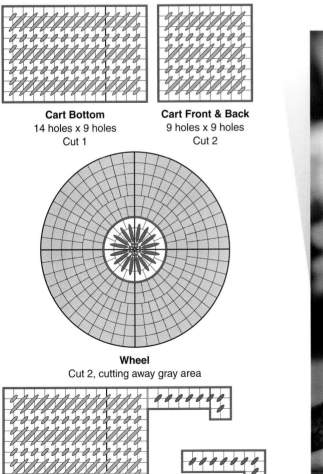

Cart Bottom
14 holes x 9 holes
Cut 1

Cart Front & Back
9 holes x 9 holes
Cut 2

Wheel
Cut 2, cutting away gray area

Cart Side
22 holes x 9 holes
Cut 2, reverse 1

Cart Handle
8 holes x 3 holes
Cut 2, reverse 1

Patchwork Hearts Place Mat

Add a cheery touch to your breakfast nook with this enchanting quilt-style place mat!

Design by Angie Arickx

TAKE NOTE

Skill Level: Beginner

Finished Size: 17⅜ inches W x 11⅜ inches L

YOU'LL NEED

- ☐ 1 (12-inch x 18-inch) sheet Darice Super Soft 7-count plastic canvas
- ☐ Uniek Needloft plastic canvas yarn as listed in color key
- ☐ #16 tapestry needle

INSTRUCTIONS

1 Cut place mat from plastic canvas according to graph.

2 Stitch right half of place mat following graph. Work bottom two stitches of Smyrna Crosses with sail blue; work top two stitches with baby blue. Turn graph and stitch left half, making sure not to repeat center two bars after turning graph.

3 Overcast with eggshell. ▧

COLOR KEY	
Plastic Canvas Yarn	**Yards**
▨ Lavender #05	10
▧ Pink #07	11
▨ Sail blue #35	28
☐ Baby blue #36	24
☐ Eggshell #39	89
▪ Lilac #45	12
Color numbers given are for Uniek Needloft plastic canvas yarn.	

Center Bars

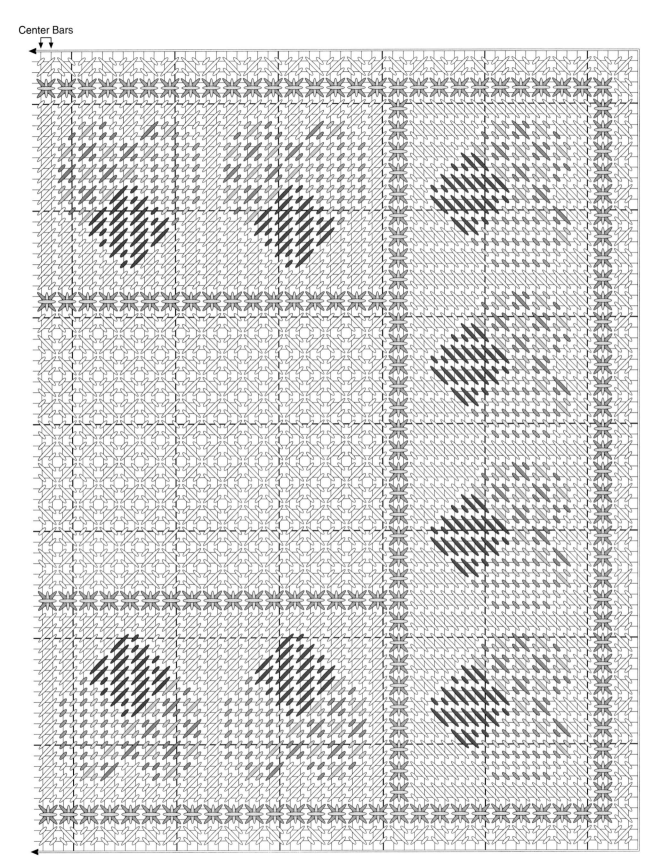

Place Mat
115 holes x 75 holes
Cut 1
Stitch right half as graphed
Turn graph and stitch left half
Do not repeat center bars

Floral Lattice Doily

Beautify and protect a wood table with this lovely doily.
Delicate embroidery adds the finishing touch!

Design by Michele Wilcox

TAKE NOTE

Skill Level: Beginner

Finished Size: 9½ inches W x 12¾ inches L

YOU'LL NEED

- ☐ 1 sheet 7-count plastic canvas
- ☐ Uniek Needloft craft cord as listed in color key
- ☐ DMC #5 pearl cotton as listed in color key
- ☐ #16 tapestry needle

INSTRUCTIONS

1 Cut plastic canvas according to graph.

2 Continental Stitch doily following graph, working uncoded areas with white Continental Stitches.

3 Overcast doily with baby blue and white following graph.

4 Work embroidery following graphs, wrapping pearl cotton around needle three times for French Knots. ▪

COLOR KEY	
Plastic Canvas Yarn	**Yards**
☐ Straw #19	6
☐ Baby blue #36	40
Uncoded areas are white #41 Continental Stitches	26
⁄ White #41 Overcasting	
#5 Pearl Cotton	
⁄ Bright canary #973 Straight Stitch	6
◔ Bright green #700 Lazy Daisy	12
● Turquoise #597 French Knot	27
● Bright green #700 French Knot	
● Medium rose #899 French Knot	2
● Bright canary #973 French Knot	
Color numbers given are for Uniek Needloft plastic canvas yarn and craft cord and DMC #5 pearl cotton.	

Doily
63 holes x 85 holes
Cut 1

Winged Wonders Napkin Cuffs

*These sparkling napkin cuffs are a unique and
decorative way to set napkins on your table.*

Designs by Joan Green

COLOR KEY

Worsted Weight Yarn		Yards
☐ Natural #8940		56
Uncoded areas are natural #8940 Continental Stitches		
1/8-Inch Metallic Needlepoint Yarn		
☐ Gold #PC1		2
☐ Pink #PC8		1
◼ Opal multi #PC9		1
◪ Peacock blue #PC12		2
▨ Fuchsia #PC13		2
☐ Light blue #PC14		2
▨ Purple #PC15		3
▨ Mother-of-pearl #PC20		1
1/16-Inch Metallic Needlepoint Yarn		
✎ Gold #PM51 Backstitch		3
○ Gold #PM51 French Knot		

Color numbers given are for Spinrite Bernat Berella "4" worsted weight yarn and Rainbow Gallery 1/8-inch-wide metallic needlepoint yarn and 1/16-inch-wide metallic needlepoint yarn.

Cuff Back
22 holes x 40 holes
Cut 4

TAKE NOTE

Skill Level: Beginner

Finished Size: 3½ inches W x 6¼ inches L

YOU'LL NEED

- ☐ 1 sheet 7-count plastic canvas
- ☐ Spinrite Bernat Berella "4" worsted weight yarn as listed in color key
- ☐ ⅛ inch-wide Plastic Canvas 7 Metallic Needlepoint Yarn by Rainbow Gallery as listed in color key
- ☐ 1/16 inch-wide Plastic Canvas 10 Metallic Needlepoint Yarn by Rainbow Gallery as listed in color key
- ☐ #16 tapestry needle

INSTRUCTIONS

1 Cut plastic canvas according to graphs.

2 Stitch pieces following graphs, working uncoded areas on fronts with natural Continental Stitches. When background stitching is completed, work gold French Knots and Backstitches with 1/16-inch metallic needlepoint yarn.

3 Using natural throughout, Overcast top edges of fronts and backs from dot to dot. With wrong sides together, Whipstitch one back to each front around remaining edges. ■

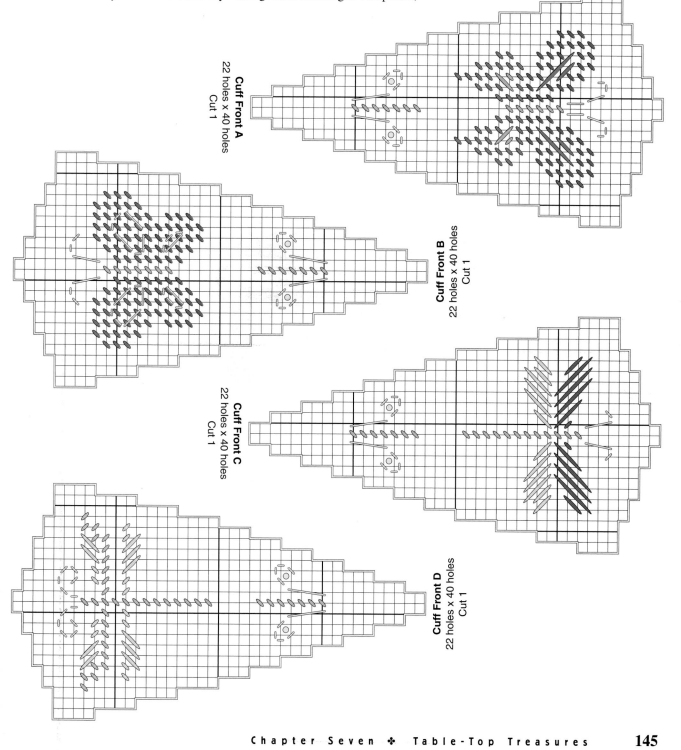

Cuff Front A
22 holes x 40 holes
Cut 1

Cuff Front B
22 holes x 40 holes
Cut 1

Cuff Front C
22 holes x 40 holes
Cut 1

Cuff Front D
22 holes x 40 holes
Cut 1

Oriental Flowers Table Set

*Put the finishing touches on your table with this three-piece set,
including a place card holder, napkin ring and flower vase.*

Designs by Celia Lange Designs

TAKE NOTE

Skill Level: Beginner

Finished Size:

Place Card Holder: 4¼ inches W x 1¾ inches H x 2 inches D

Napkin Ring: 2 inches W x 2 inches L x 2 inches in diameter

Vase: 2¾ inches W x 3⅜ inches H x ⅞ inches D

YOU'LL NEED

☐ 1 sheet 7-count plastic canvas

☐ Coats & Clark Red Heart Super Saver worsted weight yarn Art. E301 as listed in color key

☐ DMC #3 pearl cotton as listed in color key

☐ #16 tapestry needle

☐ Hot-glue gun

INSTRUCTIONS

1 Cut one each of vase front and back, two medallions and one napkin ring according to graphs.

2 Cut two 24-hole x 10-hole pieces for holder front and back, one 24-hole x 3 hole piece for holder bottom, one 24-hole x 2-hole piece for holder lip.

3 Cut two 5-hole x 27-hole pieces for vase side and one 7-hole x 5-hole piece for vase bottom.

4 Stitch vase sides and bottom and holder front, back, bottom and lip with mint Continental Stitches.

5 Stitch remaining pieces following graphs, working uncoded areas with mint Continental Stitches. Work embroidery with pearl cotton when background stitching is completed.

ASSEMBLY

1 Use mint for Overcasting and Whipstitching throughout assembly. For place card holder, Whipstitch wrong sides of front and back together along one long edge.

2 With right sides together, Whipstitch one long edge of holder bottom to bottom edge of front. With right side of lip facing out, Whipstitch holder lip to holder bottom. Overcast all remaining edges of holder and of one medallion.

3 Using photo as a guide, glue medallion to right side of holder.

4 For napkin ring, Whipstitch short edges of ring together, then Overcast remaining edges and remaining medallion. Glue medallion to ring, covering seam.

5 For vase, Whipstitch 7-hole edges of vase bottom to bottom edge of vase front and back, then Whipstitch sides to bottom, front and back; Overcast top edges. ■

COLOR KEY

Plastic Canvas Yarn	Yards
Uncoded areas are mint #366 Continental Stitches	41
⁄ Mint #366 Overcasting and Whipstitching	
#3 Pearl Cotton	
⁄ Very dark golden olive #829 Straight Stitch	2
⁄ Very dark gray green #924 Backstitch	2
⌀ Off-white #746 Lazy Daisy	5
○ Light tan #437 French Knot	2
Color numbers given are for Coats & Clark Red Heart Super Saver worsted weight yarn Art. E301 and DMC #3 pearl cotton.	

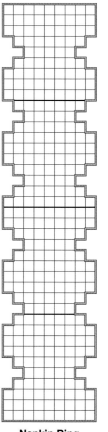

Napkin Ring
9 holes x 39 holes
Cut 1

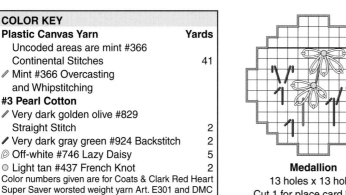

Medallion
13 holes x 13 holes
Cut 1 for place card holder
Cut 1 for napkin ring

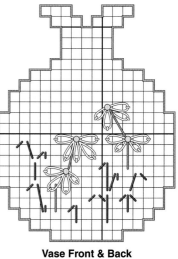

Vase Front & Back
17 holes x 22 holes
Cut 2

Sharon

Golden Wedding Ring Accents

Celebrate marriage with this set of candle holders and centerpiece.
It's perfect for 50th anniversary celebrations or weddings!

Designs by Ruby Thacker

TAKE NOTE

Skill Level: Intermediate

Finished Size:

Candle Holder: 4$\frac{3}{8}$ inches W x 4$\frac{1}{8}$ inches H x 4$\frac{1}{4}$ inches D, excluding ribbon tails and beads-on-a-string

Centerpiece: 6$\frac{7}{8}$ inches W x 5$\frac{1}{4}$ inches H x 3$\frac{1}{4}$ inches D, excluding ribbon tails and beads-on-a-string

YOU'LL NEED

- [ ] 1 sheet Darice Ultra Stiff 7-count plastic canvas
- [ ] 2 (3-inch) plastic canvas radial circles by Uniek
- [ ] Uniek Needloft craft cord as listed in color key
- [ ] #16 tapestry needle
- [ ] 3 yards $\frac{1}{4}$-inch-wide white iridescent ribbon
- [ ] 1 yard $\frac{5}{8}$-inch-wide mauve ribbon with wire edge
- [ ] 3$\frac{1}{2}$ yards $\frac{1}{8}$-inch-wide mauve satin ribbon
- [ ] 22 inches 4mm clear round bead-on-a-string
- [ ] 12 inches $\frac{1}{2}$-inch-wide gathered white lace with scalloped edges
- [ ] 2 (3$\frac{1}{4}$-inch) gold hexagon coasters/plates
- [ ] 2 (1$\frac{1}{4}$-inch) gold candle holder with $\frac{7}{8}$-inch hole
- [ ] 24 ($\frac{5}{8}$-inch) mauve ribbon roses
- [ ] 11 ($\frac{3}{8}$-inch) mauve ribbon roses
- [ ] 4 medium rose leaves
- [ ] 10 small rose leaves
- [ ] Scraps Styrofoam plastic foam
- [ ] Spanish moss
- [ ] Small dried flowers
- [ ] Hot-glue gun

PROJECT NOTE

Remove string from center of gold cord before stitching.

CANDLE HOLDERS

CUTTING & STITCHING

1 Cut two wedding rings and two bouquet holder handles from stiff plastic canvas according to graphs. Do not cut slits in rings.

2 Cut two bouquet holders from plastic canvas radial circles following graph, cutting away gray area.

3 Overcast bouquet holder handle where indicated on graph. Stitch bouquet holders following graph, overlapping two holes as indicated before stitching. Overcast top edge with white iridescent craft cord.

4 Following graphs, for each holder ring, overlap two holes and stitch. Overcast edges with solid gold.

ASSEMBLY

1 Use photo as a guide throughout assembly, insert unstitched edges of handles into bottom hole of stitched holders; glue to secure.

2 Cut two 6-inch lengths of gathered white lace; glue one length around inside top edge of each holder. Glue plastic foam scraps inside holder, then glue Spanish moss to cover scraps.

3 Glue five small rose leaves, six large ribbon roses, four small ribbon roses and dried flowers as desired in each bouquet holder.

4 Cut two 15$\frac{1}{2}$-inch lengths of $\frac{1}{4}$-inch-wide white iridescent ribbon,

four 12¼-inch lengths ⅛-inch-wide
mauve ribbon and two 6-inch lengths of
bead-on-a-string.

5 Tie each length of white ribbon in a
double bow. Tie each length of ⅛-
inch-wide mauve ribbon in a bow,
inserting one length of bead-on-a-string
through center knot of two mauve bows
before tightening bows.

6 For each bouquet holder, glue one
white bow and two mauve bows,
including one with bead-on-a-string to
front of bouquet holder above handle,
placing mauve bows on top of white bow.

7 Glue one bouquet holder to each
wedding ring. Glue one 1¼-inch
gold candle holder to gold coaster. Glue
wedding ring to coaster behind gold
candle holder.

CENTERPIECE

CUTTING & STITCHING

1 Cut two wedding rings and one base
from plastic canvas according to
graphs, cutting out slits in wedding rings.

2 Stitch and Overcast base following
graph. Stitch one centerpiece ring,
overlapping three holes; Overcast edges.

3 Stitch and Overcast all but over-
lapped holes of second centerpiece
ring, then slip slits of second ring into
slits of first ring so that unfinished ends
meet inside first ring. Complete stitching and Overcasting second ring. Glue
slits to secure.

ASSEMBLY

1 Use photo as guide throughout
assembly. Center and glue rings to
top of base.

2 Cut two 22½-inch lengths and four
8-inch lengths from both ¼-inch-
wide white iridescent ribbon and ⅛-
inch-wide mauve ribbon. Cut two 5-
inch lengths from bead-on-a-string.

3 Glue four medium rose leaves to top
of rings, placing two on each side.
Make a multi-loop bow from ⅝-inch-
wide mauve ribbon and glue to top of
rings over leaves.

4 Make bows with each 22½-inch
length of white iridescent ribbon and
each length ⅛-inch-wide mauve ribbon.

Glue bows to top, placing mauve bows
on top of white bows.

5 Glue six ⅝-inch ribbon roses, three
⅜-inch ribbon roses and small dried
flowers to top of bows as desired.

6 Make bows with two of the remaining white iridescent ribbon lengths
and two of the remaining mauve ribbon
lengths. Glue stems of three ⅝-inch ribbon roses under one wedding ring. Glue
bows and one length of bead-on-a-string
over stems.

7 Repeat step 6, placing arrangement
under second wedding ring. ■

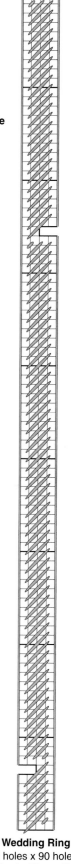

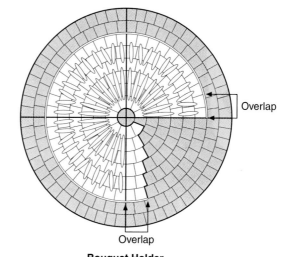

Bouquet Holder Handle
3 holes x 8 holes
Cut 2
Do not stitch

COLOR KEY	
Worsted Weight Yarn	**Yards**
▨ Solid gold #55020	22
☐ White iridescent #55033	19
Color numbers given are for Uniek Needloft craft cord.	

Overlap

Overlap

Bouquet Holder
Cut 2, cutting away gray areas

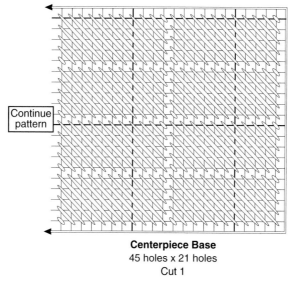

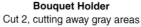

Continue
pattern

Centerpiece Base
45 holes x 21 holes
Cut 1

Wedding Ring
4 holes x 90 holes
Cut 2 without slits
for candle holders
Cut 2 with slits
for centerpiece

Pumpkin Patch Table Set

This place mat, napkin holder and napkin ring set will add a pleasant touch to your everyday dining throughout the autumn season.

Designs by Angie Arickx

TAKE NOTE

Skill Level: Beginner

Finished Size:

Place Mat: 16½ inches W x 11¾ inches L

Napkin Holder: 7 inches W x 4⅜ inches H x 2⅝ inches D

Napkin Ring: 2 inches W x 1¾ inches in diameter

YOU'LL NEED

☐ 1 (12-inch x 18-inch) sheet Darice Super Soft 7-count plastic canvas

☐ 1 sheet Darice Ultra Stiff 7-count plastic canvas

☐ Uniek Needloft plastic canvas yarn as listed in color key

☐ #16 tapestry needle

INSTRUCTIONS

1 Cut place mat and napkin ring from soft plastic canvas; cut napkin holder pieces from stiff plastic canvas according to graphs (pages 151 and 152). Cut one 45-hole x 17-hole piece from stiff plastic canvas for napkin holder bottom. Napkin holder bottom will remain unstitched.

Overlap   Overlap

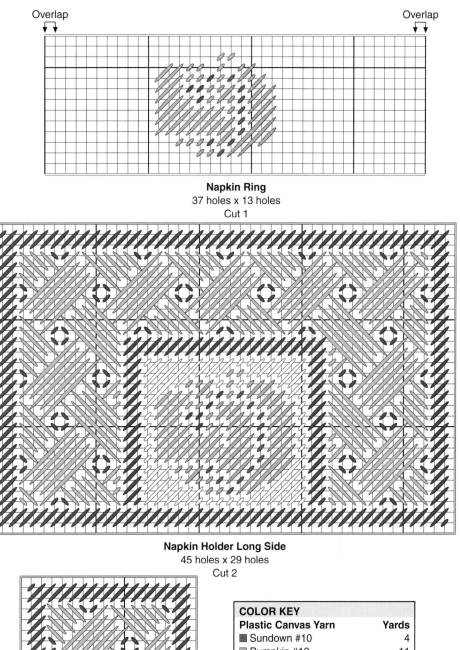

Napkin Ring
37 holes x 13 holes
Cut 1

Napkin Holder Long Side
45 holes x 29 holes
Cut 2

COLOR KEY

Plastic Canvas Yarn	Yards
■ Sundown #10	4
■ Pumpkin #12	11
□ Mint #24	11
■ Forest #29	7
□ Eggshell #39	54
■ Beige #40	77
■ Camel #43	49

Uncoded areas are eggshell
#39 Continental Stitches
Color numbers given are for Uniek Needloft
plastic canvas yarn.

2 Stitch remaining pieces following graphs. Overlap two holes of napkin ring, then stitch as graphed, working uncoded area with eggshell Continental Stitches,

3 Overcast top and bottom edges of napkin ring with eggshell.

4 Using beige throughout, Overcast place mat and top edges of holder sides. Whipstitch holder long sides to holder short sides, then Whipstitch sides to unstitched bottom. ■

Napkin Holder Short Side
17 holes x 29 holes
Cut 2

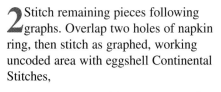

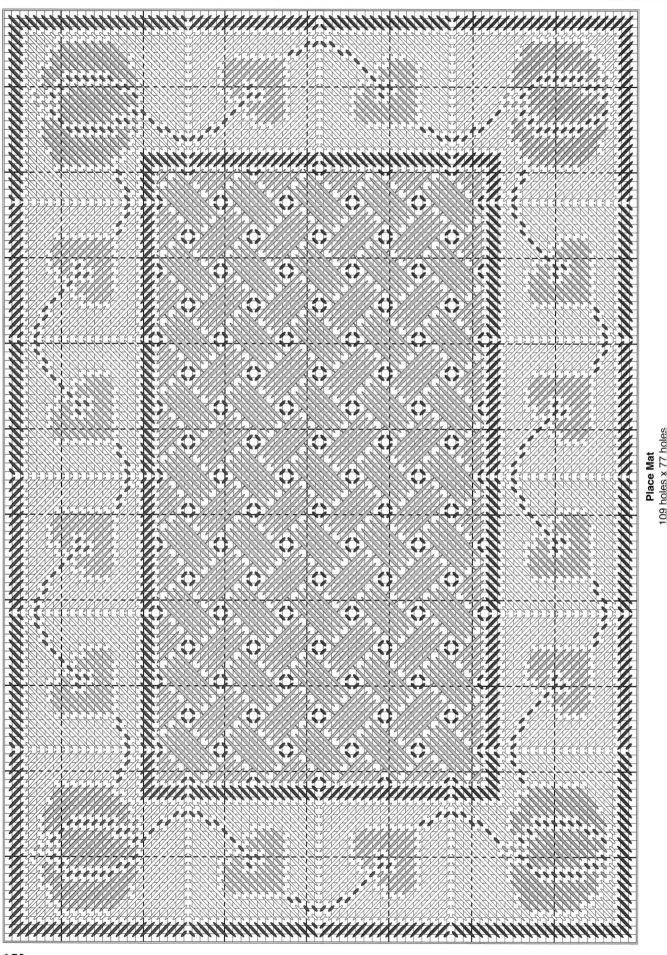

Place Mat
109 holes x 77 holes

Christmas Topiaries

Make your holiday dinner table extra-merry with this set of topiary place settings!

Designs by Vicki Blizzard

TAKE NOTE

Skill Level: Beginner

Finished Size:

Large Topiary: 2¾ inches W x 6⅜ inches H x 2 inches D

Small Topiary: 2¾ inches W x 5¾ inches H x 2 inches D

YOU'LL NEED

- ☐ 1 plastic canvas hexagon shape from Uniek
- ☐ Uniek Needloft plastic canvas yarn as listed in color key
- ☐ #16 tapestry needle
- ☐ 41 (3mm) round ruby cabochons from The Beadery
- ☐ 3 (10mm) ruby heart cabochons from The Beadery
- ☐ 3 (1⅝-inch) wooden star shapes
- ☐ 18 inches ⅛-inch dowel
- ☐ 8 inches ⅜-inch-wide red grosgrain Swiss dot ribbon
- ☐ 6 inches ⅜-inch-wide emerald grosgrain Swiss dot ribbon

- DecoArt acrylic Patio Paint: geranium red #DCP7 and pot o' gold #DCP11
- Small paintbrush
- 3 (1½-inch) terra-cotta pots
- Fine gold steel wool
- Disposable cup
- Quick-setting plaster of paris mix
- Water
- Small amount aluminum foil
- Sharp scissors
- Fine-point permanent black marker
- Jewel glue
- Hot-glue gun

CUTTING & STITCHING

1 Cut hexagon shape into six triangle shapes along dividing lines.

2 Stitch two triangles with each tree design following graph, stitching bottom edges as shown. With holly, Overcast around top of trees from dot to dot.

3 Whipstitch wrong sides of matching tree triangles together along remaining side edges.

FINISHING

1 Paint inside and outside of each terra-cotta pot with several coats of geranium red, allowing to dry thoroughly between coats.

2 Cut aluminum foil to fit inside each pot, covering hole, then place in bottom of each pot.

3 In a disposable cup, mix ½ cup plaster of paris with enough water to form pancake batter consistency. Pour mix into each pot, filling to approximately ⅛ inch from top of pot. Allow plaster to set until it begins to thicken.

4 Cut dowel into one 5½-inch and two 5-inch lengths. Insert one dowel in each pot, pushing end gently through

thickening plaster to bottom of pot, making sure it is completely vertical and not at an angle. Allow plaster to harden completely.

5 Coat top of plaster in each pot with a thick layer of jewel glue. Using photo as a guide, press small amount of fine gold steel wool around dowel into glue. Trim edges of steel wool with sharp scissors to fit inside pot, if desired.

6 Glue cabochons to fronts of trees as in photo or as desired. Glue one heart cabochon to top front of each tree. Insert one dowel in each tree, pushing dowel to top of tree. If desired, glue in place.

7 Cut emerald ribbon in half. Tie emerald and red ribbons into small bows, twisting ribbon so dotted side always faces out. Glue bow to front of each pot with hot glue.

8 Paint both sides of each star with pot o' gold paint; allow to dry. With permanent marker, Write desired name on each star; Insert one star in top opening of each tree. ∎

COLOR KEY

Plastic Canvas Yarn	Yards
■ Holly #27	12
□ White #41	6

Color numbers given are for Uniek Needloft plastic canvas yarn.

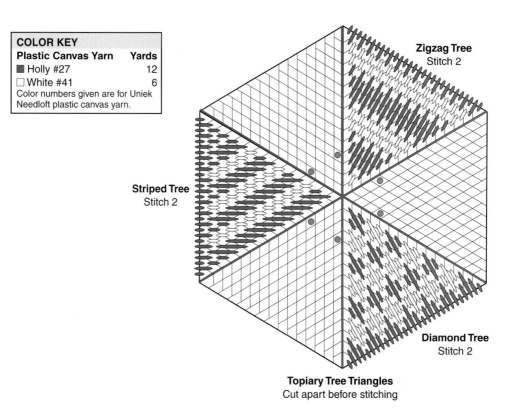

Zigzag Tree
Stitch 2

Striped Tree
Stitch 2

Diamond Tree
Stitch 2

Topiary Tree Triangles
Cut apart before stitching

Sweet-Scents Sensations

Treat yourself to an enriching and relaxing session of stitching!
Each of these handsome projects, from potpourri holders to
perfumed sachets, will soothe your senses with their
lovely designs and sweet aromas!

Love 'n' Fragrance Box

Heart-shaped plastic canvas makes this box easy to stitch and assemble.
The top is open for displaying your favorite potpourri.
Photo on page 155.

Design by Carol Dace

TAKE NOTE

Skill Level: Intermediate

Finished Size: 6½ inches W x 6 inches L x 8¾ inches H, including bow

YOU'LL NEED

- 1 sheet Uniek Quick-Count 7-count plastic canvas
- 2 (6-inch) plastic canvas heart shapes by Uniek
- Worsted weight yarn as listed in color key
- #16 tapestry needle
- 27 inches ⅜-inch-wide cream double sided satin ribbon
- 45 inches ⅛-inch-wide cream double sided satin ribbon
- 1-inch gold heart charm or button
- 2 (5-inch) lengths thin white wire
- Tacky glue
- Hot-glue gun

INSTRUCTIONS

1 Cut plastic canvas according to graphs, cutting away gray areas on heart graphs.

2 Using light camel for all stitching, stitch pieces following graphs, using two-yard lengths for Gobelin Stitches on top and sides.

3 Overcast outside "lacy" edges of box top. Whipstitch sides to inside edges of top, then Whipstitch sides together. Whipstitch bottom to sides.

4 Using photo as a guide through step 6, make a six-loop bow with ⅜-inch-wide ribbon; fasten in the middle with one length of wire.

5 Using tacky glue, glue ⅛-inch-wide ribbon around center row of stitches on box sides. Make a six-loop bow with remaining ribbon; fasten in the middle with remaining length of wire.

6 Using hot glue, glue large and small bows to top where indicated on graph; glue heart charm between bows. ▪

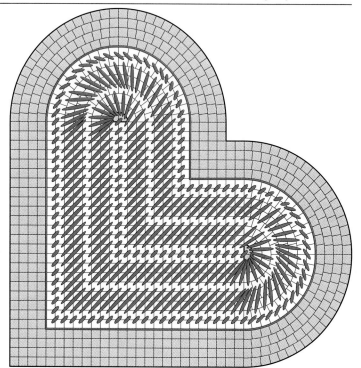

Box Bottom
Cut 1, cutting away gray area

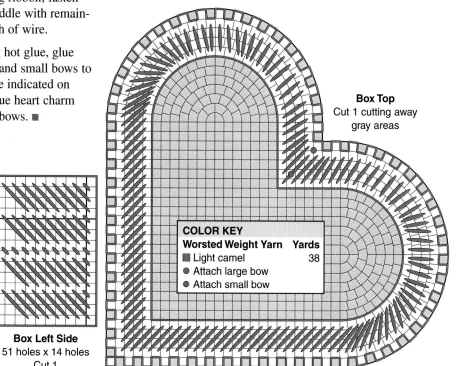

Box Top
Cut 1 cutting away gray areas

COLOR KEY	
Worsted Weight Yarn	**Yards**
▪ Light camel	38
● Attach large bow	
● Attach small bow	

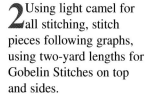

Continue pattern

Continue pattern

Box Right Side
51 holes x 14 holes
Cut 1

Box Left Side
51 holes x 14 holes
Cut 1

Sparkling Soap Boxes

*Fill these sparkling boxes with decorative soaps and
bubble bath beads for a special gift!*

Designs by Susan Leinberger

TAKE NOTE

Skill Level: Beginner

Finished Size:

English Lavender: 3¼ inches W x 4½ inches H x 2 inches D

Evening Primrose: 4½ inches W x 2¼ inches H x 3⅛ inches D

YOU'LL NEED

☐ 2 sheets white 7-count plastic canvas

☐ Uniek Needloft metallic craft cord as listed in color key

☐ Uniek Needloft Frizette craft cord as listed in color key

☐ Uniek Needloft metallic piping craft cord as listed in color key

☐ #16 tapestry needle

☐ 2 (8mm) pearl buttons with shanks

☐ Sewing needle and clear nylon thread

INSTRUCTIONS

1 Cut plastic canvas according to graphs. Cut one 18-hole x 12-hole piece for English lavender box bottom and one 27-hole x 19-hole piece for evening primrose box bottom. Box bottoms will remain unstitched.

2 Stitch remaining pieces following graphs. Center top of English lavender lid top will remain unstitched.

3 When background stitching is completed, work Backstitches, Straight Stitches, Lazy Daisy Stitches and French Knots.

4 With sewing needle and clear nylon thread, attach buttons to box fronts where indicated on graphs.

5 For English lavender box, using soft purple through step 6, Whipstitch front and back to sides, then Whipstitch front, back and sides to bottom; Overcast top edges of front and sides only.

6 Whipstitch lid long side to lid short sides, then Whipstitch sides to front and side edges of lid top. Overcast remaining edges of lid sides, then Whipstitch back edge of lid top to top edge box back.

7 For evening primrose box, repeat steps 5 and 6 using soft pink.

8 For box closure on each box, thread a length of white iridescent cord from front to back through holes indicated on lid front graphs. Adjust length to fit over button; knot on back and trim ends. ◼

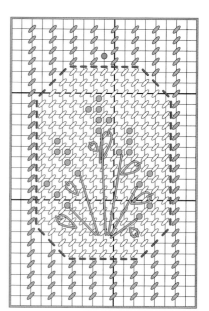

English Lavender Box Front
18 holes x 27 holes
Cut 1

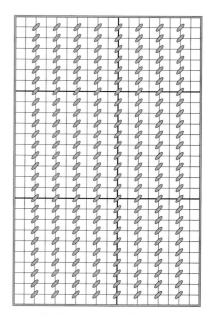

English Lavender Box Back
18 holes x 27 holes
Cut 1

COLOR KEY
ENGLISH LAVENDER BOX

Metallic Craft Cord	Yards
☐ White iridescent #55033	5
Frizette Craft Cord	
▨ Soft purple #55025	15
⟋ Soft green #55023 Straight Stitch	2
⟢ Soft green #55023 Lazy Daisy	
● Soft purple #55025 French Knot	
Metallic Piping	
◼ Solid purple #55030	2
⟋ Solid purple #55030 Backstitch	
● Attach button	
○ Attach cord for closure	

Color numbers given are for Uniek metallic craft cord, frizette craft cord and metallic piping cord.

English Lavender Box Lid Front
20 holes x 2 holes
Cut 1

English Lavender Box Lid Side
13 holes x 2 holes
Cut 2

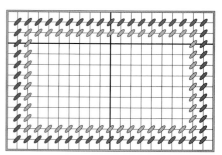

English Lavender Box Side
12 holes x 27 holes
Cut 2

English Lavender Box Lid Top
20 holes x 13 holes
Cut 1

COLOR KEY
EVENING PRIMROSE BOX

Metallic Craft Cord	Yards
Uncoded areas on box lid top are white iridescent #55033 Continental Stitches	5

Frizette Craft Cord

☐ Soft pink #55024	25
✐ Soft green #55023 Straight Stitch	1
⬭ Soft green #55023 Lazy Daisy	
○ Soft pink #55024 French Knot	

Metallic Piping

☐ Solid magenta #55032	2
✐ Solid magenta #55032 Backstitch	
● Solid magenta #55032 French Knot	
● Attach button	
● Attach cord for closure	

Color numbers given are for Uniek metallic craft cord, frizette craft cord and metallic piping.

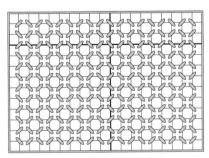

Evening Primrose Box Lid Top
29 holes x 20 holes
Cut 1

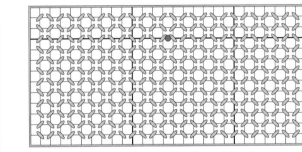

Evening Primrose Box Front & Back
27 holes x 13 holes
Cut 2

Evening Primrose Box Lid Front
29 holes x 2 holes
Cut 1

Evening Primrose Box Lid Side
20 holes x 2 holes
Cut 2

Evening Primrose Box Side
19 holes x 13 holes
Cut 2

Dainty Basket Door Decor

Lovely hues of lavender (or your favorite color) make this dainty project a perfect accent for the bedroom or bathroom.

Design by Joan Green

TAKE NOTE

Skill Level: Beginner

Finished Size: 7¼ inches W x 9 inches H x 1⅛ inches D

YOU'LL NEED

- ⅔ sheet 7-count plastic canvas
- Coats & Clark Red Heart Classic worsted weight yarn Art. E267 as listed in color key
- #16 tapestry needle
- 1½-inch pale pink tassel
- ½-inch orchid ribbon rose with leaves
- 12 inches gold glitter stem
- 12 inches 20-gauge green cloth covered wire
- Pencil
- Potpourri
- Fabric glue

INSTRUCTIONS

1 Cut plastic canvas according to graph.

2 Stitch basket front following graph. When background stitching is completed, work off-white French Knots. Basket back will remain unstitched so more fragrance will come through basket.

3 Using off-white, Overcast top edges of both front and back around curves from blue dot to blue dot. With lily pink, tack tassel to backside of front where indicated on graph, allowing tassel to hang freely.

4 With off-white, Whipstitch wrong sides of front and back together along remaining top edges. With light plum, Whipstitch around remaining side and bottom edges, making sure not to catch tassel in Whipstitching.

5 Using photo as a guide through step 6, glue ribbon rose to center top front. To secure, add a dab of glue to light plum yarn where tassel is attached.

6 Twist glitter stem and green wire together. Then loosely wrap around pencil. Curve ends to fit under Whipstitched edges at center top; glue in place.

7 Pack basket with potpourri. ∎

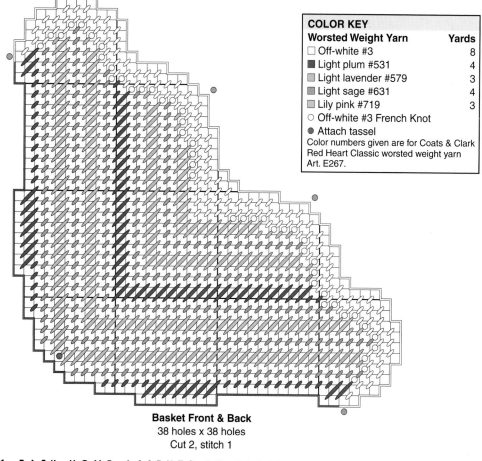

COLOR KEY

Worsted Weight Yarn	Yards
☐ Off-white #3	8
◼ Light plum #531	4
▦ Light lavender #579	3
▦ Light sage #631	4
▦ Lily pink #719	3
○ Off-white #3 French Knot	
● Attach tassel	

Color numbers given are for Coats & Clark Red Heart Classic worsted weight yarn Art. E267.

Basket Front & Back
38 holes x 38 holes
Cut 2, stitch 1

Butterfly Wall Pocket

Decorated with an exquisite butterfly, this unique wall hanging is a lacy pocket for holding your favorite potpourri!

Design by Janelle Marie Giese

TAKE NOTE

Skill Level: Intermediate

Finished Size: 7½ inches W x 9⅞ inches H x 1⅛ inches D, excluding tassels

YOU'LL NEED

- ☐ 2 sheets Uniek Quick-Count black 7-count plastic canvas
- ☐ Coats & Clark Red Heart Classic worsted weight yarn Art. E267 as listed in color key
- ☐ Kreinik Heavy (#32) Braid as listed in color key
- ☐ Kreinik Medium (#16) Braid as listed in color key
- ☐ Kreinik Tapestry (#12) Braid as listed in color key
- ☐ DMC #3 pearl cotton as listed in color key
- ☐ #16 tapestry needle
- ☐ 7-inch x 8-inch piece off-white lace fabric or tulle
- ☐ 2 (3-inch) black tassels
- ☐ Sawtooth hanger
- ☐ Thick white glue

INSTRUCTIONS

1 Cut plastic canvas according to graphs (page 164). Cut one 49-hole x 56-hole piece for pocket back and one 7-hole x 49-hole piece for pocket bottom.

2 Stitch back and bottom with black Continental Stitches. Using black pearl cotton, center and sew sawtooth hanger to right side of back about 6 holes down from top edge.

3 Stitch front and sides following graphs, working uncoded areas on front with black Continental Stitches and attaching bottom piece to front at Whipstitch line while stitching front.

4 Using black yarn throughout, Overcast openings on front with black. Overcast lower portion of sides and bottom edge on front from blue dot to blue dot, Whipstitching center bottom edge of front pocket to pocket bottom while Overcasting.

5 Work embroidery on front and sides following graphs. Whipstitch sides to front with black yarn.

6 Using photo as a guide, for antennae, thread a 3½- to 3¾-inch length of black pearl cotton through yarn on backside of head, allowing ends to extend on each side of "nose." Coat ends with thick white glue and allow to dry upside down so antennae will dry upward.

7 When dry, glue lace fabric or tulle to backside of front behind openings. Allow to dry.

8 With black yarn, Whipstitch back to sides and bottom, then Overcast top edges of pocket.

9 Attach tassels to front where indicated on graph with black pearl cotton. ▪

Graphs on page 164

COLOR KEY	
Worsted Weight Yarn	**Yards**
▨ Medium clay #280	1
☐ Light sage #631	19
▨ Medium sage #632	4
■ Dark sage #633	13
■ Country blue #822	1
Uncoded areas are black #12 Continental Stitches	70
⁄ Black #12 Overcasting and Whipstiching	
◎ Light sage #631 French Knot	
Heavy (#32) Braid	
▨ Peacock #085	
Medium (#16) Braid	
⁄ Vintage verdigris #154V Backstitch and Straight Stitch	7
Tapestry (#12) Braid	
⁄ Sky blue #014 Backstitch and Straight Stitch	2
#3 Pearl Cotton	
⁄ Black #310 Backstitch and Straight Stitch	
⁄ Light old gold #676 Straight Stitch	1
⁄ Light beige gray #822 Backstitch and Straight Stitch	2
◎ Light old gold #676 French Knot	
⁄ Whipstitch to pocket bottom	
● Attach tassel	
Color numbers given are for Coats & Clark Red Heart Classic worsted weight yarn Art. E267, Kreinik Heavy (#32) Braid, Medium (#16) Braid and Tapestry (#12) Braid and DMC #3 pearl cotton.	

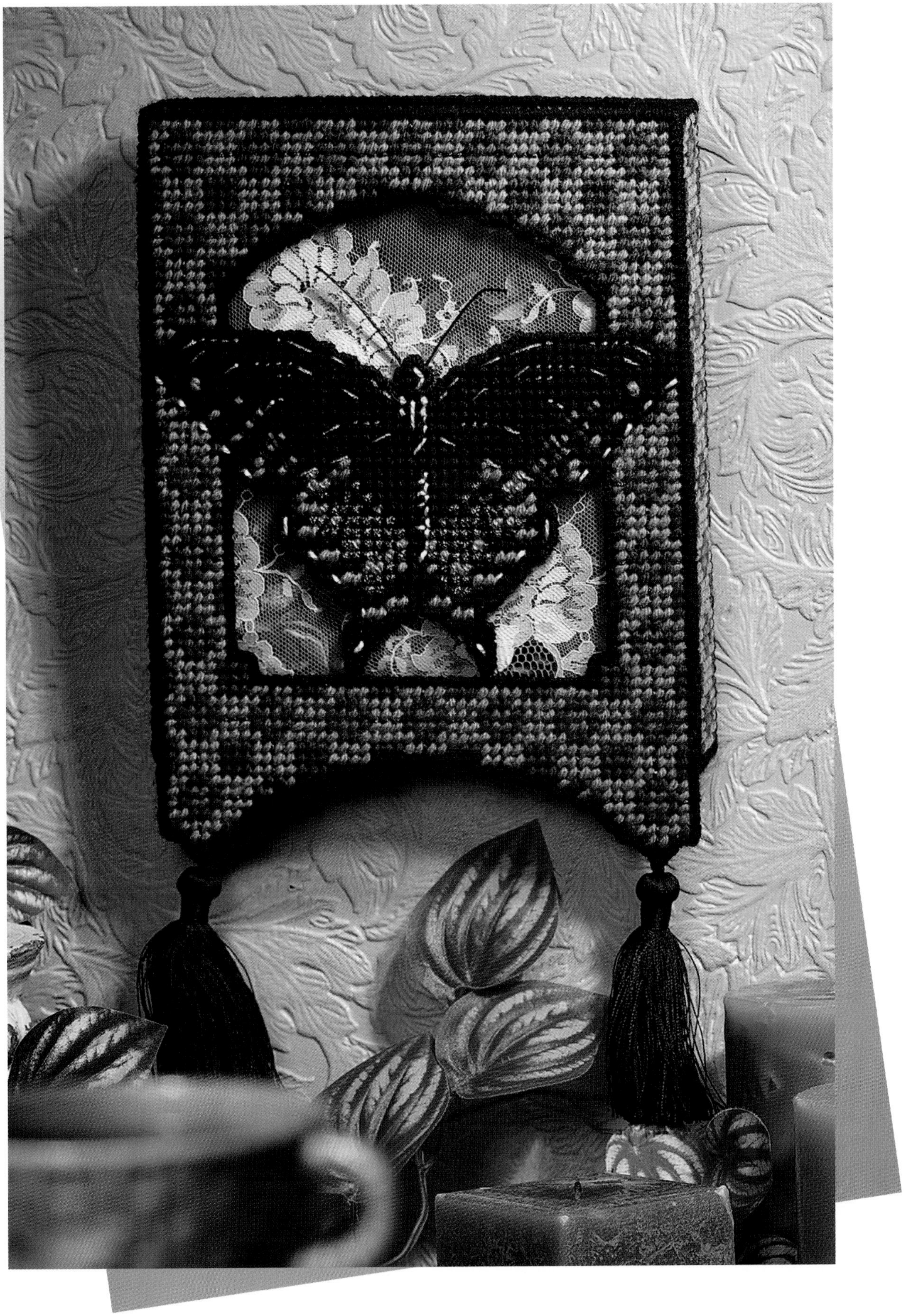

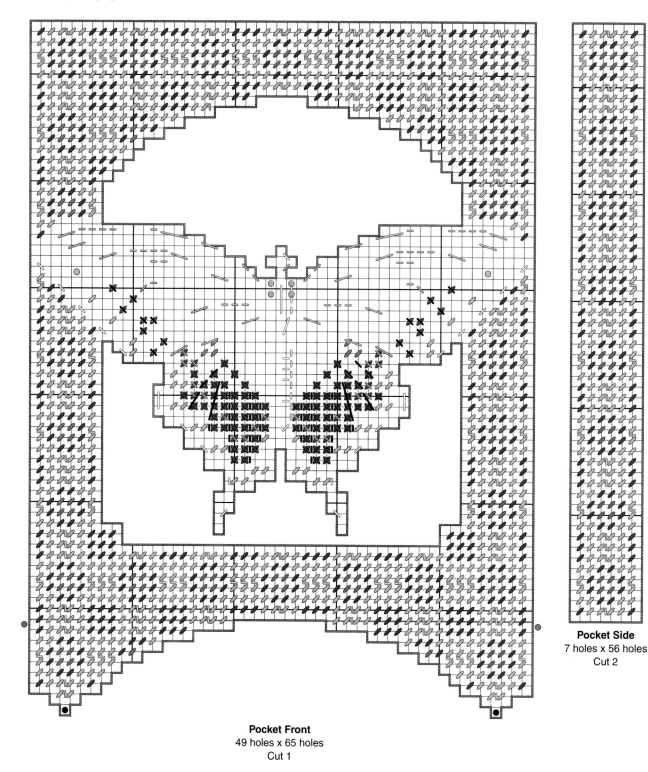

Pocket Front
49 holes x 65 holes
Cut 1

Pocket Side
7 holes x 56 holes
Cut 2

Celestial Box

Perfect for relaxing at bedtime, this celestial project will soothe away the cares of the day with aromatic potpourri!

Design by Susan Leinberger

O TAKE NOTE

Skill Level: Beginner

Finished Size: 4 inches W x 2¼ inches H x 4 inches D

YOU'LL NEED

- ☐ 1 sheet Uniek Quick-Count 7-count plastic canvas
- ☐ Uniek Needloft plastic canvas yarn as listed in color key
- ☐ Uniek Needloft metallic piping craft cord as listed in color key
- ☐ #16 tapestry needle

INSTRUCTIONS

1 Cut plastic canvas according to graphs (page 172). Box bottom will remain unstitched.

2 Stitch remaining pieces following graphs, working uncoded areas on box top with dark royal Continental Stitches. Overcast inside edges of lid top following graph.

3 Work embroidery with yarn and metallic piping following graphs.

4 Using dark royal throughout, Whipstitch box sides to box corners, then Whipstitch sides and corners to box bottom; Overcast top edges. Whipstitch lid sides to lid corners, then Whipstitch sides and corners to lid top; Overcast bottom edges. ■

Graphs on page 172

Quick Sachets

Designed with a hardanger look, this set of three
aromatic sachets is easy to stitch and pleasant to share!

Designs by Celia Lange Designs

TAKE NOTE

Skill Level: Beginner

Finished Size:

Blue Sachet: 4 inches W x 4 inches H diagonally, excluding hanger

Pink Sachet: 3½ inches W x 3½ H diagonally, excluding hanger

Mauve Sachet: 4⅜ inches W x 4⅜ inches H diagonally, excluding hanger

YOU'LL NEED

- ⅓ sheet each 10-count plastic canvas: pink, light blue and dusty rose
- DMC #3 pearl cotton as listed in color key
- #22 tapestry needle
- 17 (3mm) white peal beads
- 8 (4mm) light blue pearls
- 36 (4mm) dark pink pearls
- Beading needle
- Sewing thread: light pink, light blue and mauve
- Small amount tulle: light pink, light blue and mauve
- 7 inches ⅛-inch-wide light blue satin ribbon
- 7 inches ⅛-inch-wide light pink satin ribbon
- 8 inches ⅛-inch-wide mauve satin ribbon
- Potpourri
- Fabric glue

INSTRUCTIONS

1 Cut plastic canvas according to graphs. Using matching colors, cut tulle same size as each front and back.

2 Stitch pieces following graphs, beginning and ending with each segment of stitching. Do not run pearl cotton across unworked areas because it will show.

3 With beading needle and matching thread, attach pearls to sachet fronts only where indicated on graphs.

4 For each sachet, place both pieces of matching tulle between front and back. With adjacent colors, Whipstitch wrong sides of fronts and backs together, catching tulle while Whipstitching, forming a ½ inch hanging loop at one corner of each sachet and filling with potpourri before closing.

5 Trim any tulle as necessary showing along outside edges. Tie each length of ribbon in a bow and glue to front of matching sachet at top corner just under hanging loop. ■

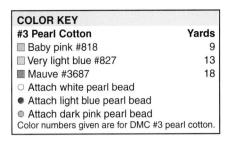

COLOR KEY

#3 Pearl Cotton	Yards
☐ Baby pink #818	9
☐ Very light blue #827	13
▨ Mauve #3687	18
○ Attach white pearl bead	
● Attach light blue pearl bead	
● Attach dark pink pearl bead	

Color numbers given are for DMC #3 pearl cotton.

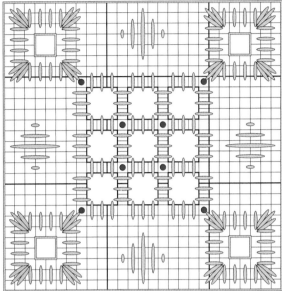

Blue Sachet
27 holes x 27 holes
Cut 2 from light blue

Pink Sachet
25 holes x 25 holes
Cut 2 from pink

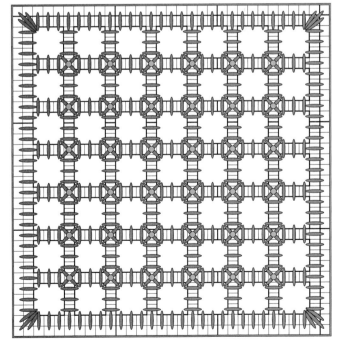

Mauve Sachet
31 holes x 31 holes
Cut 2 from dusty rose

Antique Purses

Stitch both of these lovely vintage-style purses for a lovely display in your bedroom or bathroom. Each can hold a small packet of potpourri!

Designs by Ronda Bryce

TAKE NOTE

Skill Level: Beginner

Finished Size: 5⅞ inches W x 8⅝ inches H x ¾ inches D

YOU'LL NEED

Each Purse

- □ 1 sheet black 7-count plastic canvas
- □ Coats & Clark Red Heart Super Saver worsted weight yarn Art. E301 as listed in color key
- □ Uniek Needloft metallic craft cord as listed in color key
- □ #16 tapestry needle
- □ 6 inches 2-inch-wide black fringe
- □ Sewing needle and black sewing thread
- □ ¾-inch round Velcro hook-and-loop fastener

Black Purse

- □ 6 Tiny Victorian Reproductions buttons #101 from Dress It Up Victorian Miniature Buttons by Jesse James Co.

Burgundy Purse

- □ Caron International Victorian Christmas Gold 4-ply yarn as listed in color key
- □ 89 (4mm) white pearl beads
- □ 3 (½-inch) white ribbon roses with leaves

INSTRUCTIONS

1 Cut pieces from plastic canvas according to graphs (this page and pages 170 and 171).

2 Stitch pieces following graphs, working black purse back with black/gold as graphed. Stitch burgundy purse back replacing black/gold with gold. *Note: Only the clasp at top of purse backs are stitched. Purse backs below clasp will remain unstitched.*

3 Overcast top edges of purse fronts and backs from dot to dot following graphs.

4 Using sewing needle and black thread throughout, attach beads to burgundy purse and buttons to black purse where indicated on graphs. Evenly space and attach roses to black area at top of burgundy purse front (see photo).

5 Using black throughout, for each purse, Whipstitch sides to bottom, forming one long strip. Whipstitch front and back to bottom and sides. Overcast top edges of sides.

6 Using 18 inches black/gold for black purse and 18 inches gold for burgundy purse, thread ends of cord on purse back from inside to outside through holes indicated on graph; knot at desired length.

7 For each purse, using sewing needle and black sewing thread throughout, stitch fringe to purse back just above bottom edge, turning raw edges under to fit. Stitch round hook-and-loop fastener pieces inside center top of purse front and back. ■

COLOR KEY	
BURGUNDY PURSE	
Worsted Weight Yarn	**Yards**
■ Black #312	15
4-Ply Yarn	
■ Cranberry #1900	8
Craft Cord	
▨ Gold #55001	5
○ Attach pearl	
● Attach cord handle	
Color numbers givern are for Coats & Clark Red Heart Super Saver worsted weight yarn Art. E301, Caron International Victorian Christmas Gold 4-ply yarn and Uniek Needloft craft cord.	

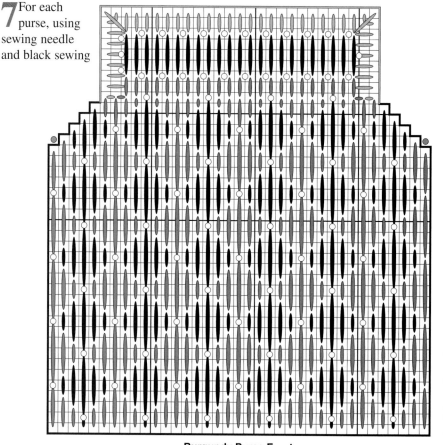

Burgundy Purse Front
37 holes x 40 holes
Cut 1

Burgundy Purse Bottom
37 holes x 4 holes
Cut 1

COLOR KEY	
BURGUNDY PURSE	
Worsted Weight Yarn	**Yards**
■ Black #312	15
4-Ply Yarn	
■ Cranberry #1900	8
Craft Cord	
▨ Gold #55001	5
○ Attach pearl	
● Attach cord handle	
Color numbers givern are for Coats & Clark Red Heart Super Saver worsted weight yarn Art. E301, Caron International Victorian Christmas Gold 4-ply yarn and Uniek Needloft craft cord.	

Burgundy Purse Side
4 holes x 27 holes
Cut 2

COLOR KEY	
BLACK PURSE	
Worsted Weight Yarn	**Yards**
■ Black #312	25
Craft Cord	
▨ Gold #55001	4
■ Black/gold #55009	5
○ Attach button	
● Attach cord handle	
Color numbers given are for Coats & Clark Red Heart Super Saver worsted weight yarn Art. E301 and Uniek Needloft craft cord.	

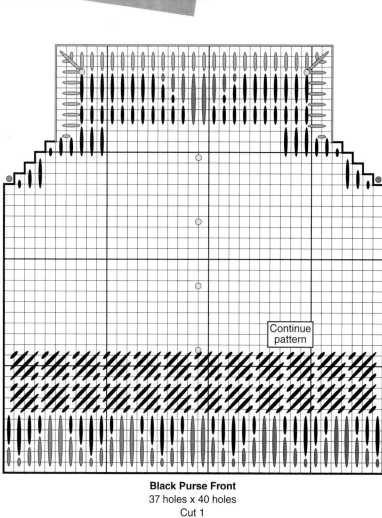

Continue pattern

Black Purse Front
37 holes x 40 holes
Cut 1

Black Purse Side
4 holes x 27 holes
Cut 2

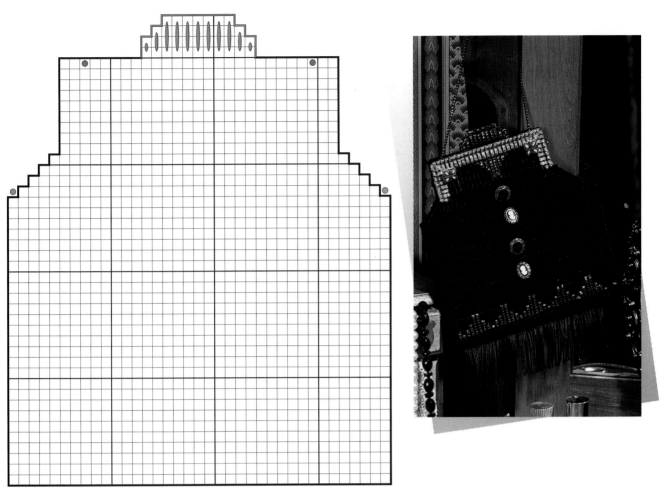

Purse Back
37 holes x 44 holes
Cut 1 for each purse
Stitch black purse as graphed
Stitch burgundy purse replacing
black/gold with gold

Black Purse Bottom
37 holes x 4 holes
Cut 1

Tips & Techniques

I save all my scraps of yarn about 2" long or longer and keep them in a bag. When we take a trip, I take along the bag and some plastic canvas squares and use the scraps to stitch coasters with the Texas Lone Star design. I usually fill in the background with off-white or a fisherman color.
—*Betty Werline, Texas*

I recently found an old set of plastic canvas coasters. Instead of having felt glued on the back, they had ⅛"-thick cork glued on. The cork not only reinforces the plastic canvas, but it also really soaks up moisture. Now I use cork to back all my coasters.
—*Kendra Scott, Texas*

When labeling items for a bazaar sale, I found self-stick labels don't work very well. Instead, I use scraps of yarn to tie a small label cut from an index card to the project. I write the item name and price on the label. Thread yarn through item and hole punched in card for a secure label.
—*Beverly Riddle, Indiana*

Keep a pair of nail clippers with your supplies for snipping off corners and nubs. They snip evenly without cutting through the bar.
—*Synethia Nelson, New York*

To keep your yarn from sticking together and tangling from static electricity, just slide your yarn through a folded fabric softener sheet. No more tangles, and you can use the sheet again and again!
—*Alice M. McDuff, Florida*

When stitching with metallic thread, I use one needle size larger than I usually use with yarn stitching. Because the eye is larger, the thread doesn't catch or fray so easily. Works great!
—*Sue Wiener, Florida*

When you are making magnets for a craft sale, make one out of 7-count plastic canvas and another out of 10-count canvas. I've made projects out of both and sell more than I can make!
—*Sharon Adkins, Michigan*

Celestial Box
Pattern continued from page 165

Box Lid Corner
6 holes x 3 holes
Cut 4

COLOR KEY	
Plastic Canvas Yarn	**Yards**
■ Dark royal #48	27
Uncoded areas are dark royal #48 Continental Stitches	
╱ Dark royal #48 Backstitch and Straight Stitch	
● Dark royal #48 French Knot	
Metallic Piping	
▢ Solid gold #55020	8
▢ Solid silver #55021	8
╱ Solid gold #55020 Backstitch and Straight Stitch	
╱ Solid silver #55021 Backstitch and Straight Stitch	
Color numbers given are for Uniek Needloft plastic canvas yarn and metallic piping.	

Box Corner
6 holes x 12 holes
Cut 4

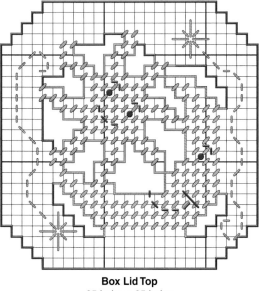

Box Lid Top
25 holes x 25 holes
Cut 1

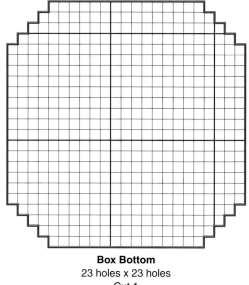

Box Bottom
23 holes x 23 holes
Cut 1
Do not stitch

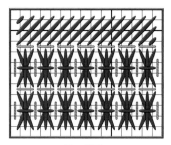

Box Side
15 holes x 12 holes
Cut 4

Box Lid Side
17 holes x 3 holes
Cut 4

Special Thanks

We would like to acknowledge and thank the following designers whose original work has been published in this collection. We appreciate and value their creativity and dedication to designing quality plastic canvas projects!

Angie Arickx
Butterfly Plant Poke, Christmas Cottage, Country Cottage, English Cottage, Hearts & Lace, Hearty Welcome, Patchwork Hearts Place Mat, Pumpkin Patch Table Set, Peek-a-Boo Bunnies Basket, Quilt-Style Photo Cube, Springtime Tissue Topper, Strawberry Patch, Teddy Bear Love Frame

Vicki Blizzard
Christmas Topiaries

Ronda Bryce
Antique Purses

Judy Collishaw
Classic Car Coasters, Country Hearts & Bears, Silly Scarecrows Wreath

Mary T. Cosgrove
Harvest Favor Cart, Holiday Gift Bag, Life on the Farm

Carol Dace
Love 'n' Fragrance Box

Darla J. Fanton
Welcome Friends

Janelle Marie Giese
Baby's First Christmas, Baby Photo Bank, Butterfly Wall Pocket, Butterfly Wind Chime, Elegant Music Box, Garden Entrance, Hummingbird Hut Wind Chime, King's Castle, Victorian Armoire

Joan Green
Anchor's Aweigh, Dainty Basket Door Decor, Family Photo Box, Golden Anchors, Winged Wonders Napkin Cuffs

Robin Howard-Will
Granny Squares Tissue Topper, Summertime Stitching

J. Sammi Johnson
Gingerbread Candy House

Joyce Keklock
Friendly Froggy Door Hanger

Celia Lange Designs
Bunny & Chick Mini Bags; Flower Box Door Chime; Fresh Eggs Doorstop; Ice Castle; I Love Gardening; Japanese Kimonos; Oriental Flowers Table Set; Quick Sachets; Sand, Surf & Sails; Textured Doorstop; Tiered Birdhouse

Susan Leinberger
Celestial Box, Sparkling Soap Boxes

Lee Lindeman
Autumn Leaves, Country Time Wind Chime, Down-on-the-Farm Fun, Dreamland Angel, Frieda Froggy, Rosebud Gazebo, Polly Pumpkin & Callie Cat Centerpieces, Turkey Basket

Alida Macor
Quilt Block Stars

Nancy Marshall
Flowers 'n' Checks, Wee Ones Frames

Laura Scott
Spools & Buttons

Ruby Thacker
Golden Wedding Ring Accents, Grand Slam Coasters, Star-Spangled Welcome

Michele Wilcox
Floral Lattice Doily

Linda Wyszynski
Victorian Bouquet

STITCH Guide

Use the following diagrams to expand your plastic canvas stitching skills. For each diagram, bring needle up through canvas at the red number one and go back down through the canvas at the red number two. The second stitch is numbered in green. Always bring needle up through the canvas at odd numbers and take it back down through the canvas at the even numbers.

Background Stitches

The following stitches are used for filling in large areas of canvas. The Continental Stitch is the most commonly used stitch. Other stitches, such as the Condensed Mosaic and Scotch Stitch, fill in large areas of canvas more quickly than the Continental Stitch because their stitches cover a larger area of canvas.

Continental Stitch

Condensed Mosaic

Running Stitch

Cross Stitch

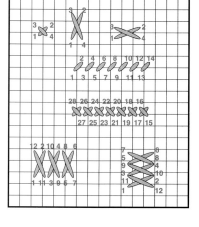

Alternating Continental

Long Stitch

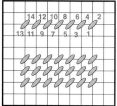

Slanting Gobelin

Scotch Stitch

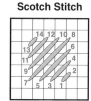

Embroidery Stitches

These stitches are worked on top of a stitched area to add detail to the project. Embroidery stitches are usually worked with one strand of yarn, several strands of pearl cotton or several strands of embroidery floss.

Lattice Stitch

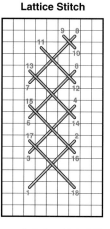

Chain Stitch

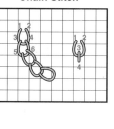

Straight Stitch

Fly Stitch

Couching

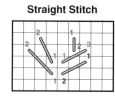

Backstitch

Stitch Guide   Stitch Guide   Stitch Guide   Stitch Guide   Stitch Guide

Embroidery Stitches

French Knot

Bring needle up through canvas.

Wrap yarn around needle 2 or 3 times, depending on desired size of knot; take needle back through canvase through same hole.

Lazy Daisy

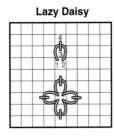

Bring yarn needle up through canvas, then back down in same hole, leaving a small loop.

Then, bring needle up inside loop; take needle back down through canvas on other side of loop.

Loop Stitch or Turkey Loop Stitch

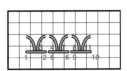

The top diagram shows this stitch left intact. This is an effective stitch for giving a project dimensional hair. The bottom diagram demonstrates the cut loop stitch. Because each stitch is anchored, cutting it will not cause the stitches to come out. A group of cut loop stitches gives a fluffy, soft look and feel to your project.

Specialty Stitches

The following stitches can be worked either on top of a previously stitched area or directly onto the canvas. Like the embroidery stitches, these too add wonderful detail and give your stitching additional interest and texture.

Diamond Eyelet

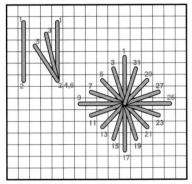

For each stitch, bring needle up at odd numbers around outside and take needle down through canvas at center hole.

Smyrna Cross

Satin Stitches

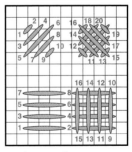

This stitch gives a "padded" look to your work.

Finishing Stitches

Overcast/Whipstitch

Overcasting and Whipstitching are used to finish the outer edges of the canvas. Overcasting is done to finish one edge at a time. Whipstitch is used to stitch two or more pieces of canvas together along on edge. For both Overcasting and Whipstitching, work one stitch in each hole along straight edges and inside corners, and two or three stitches in outside corners.

Lark's Head Knot

The Lark's Head Knot is used for a fringe edge or for attaching a hanging loop.

Stitch Guide   Stitch Guide   Stitch Guide   Stitch Guide   Stitch Guide

Buyer's Guide

When looking for a specific material, first check your local craft and retail stores. If you are unable to locate a product locally, contact the manufacturers listed below for the closest retail source in your area or a mail-order source.

The Beadery
P.O. Box 178
Hope Valley, RI 02832
(401) 539-2432

Caron International
Customer Service
P.O. Box 222
Washington, NC 27889
(800) 868-9194
www.caron.com

Coats & Clark
Consumer Service
P.O. Box 12229
Greenville, SC 29612-0229
(800) 648-1479
www.coatsandclark.com

Creative Beginnings
P.O. Box 1330
Morro Bay, CA 93442
(800) 367-1739

Darice
Mail-order source:
Bolek's
P.O. Box 465
330 N. Tuscarawas Ave.
Dover, OH 44622
(330) 364-8878

DecoArt
P.O. Box 386
Stanford, KY 40484
(800) 367-3047
www.decoart.com

DMC Corp.
Hackensack Ave. Bldg. 10A
South Kearny, NJ 07032-4688
(800) 275-4117
www.dmc-usa.com

Jesse James & Co.
615 N. New St.
Allentown, PA 18102
(610) 435-7899

Kreinik Mfg. Co. Inc.
3106 Timanus Ln., #101
Baltimore, MD 21244-2871
(800) 537-2166

**Kunin Felt Co./
Foss Mfg. Co. Inc.**
P.O. Box 5000
Hampton, NH 03842-5000
(800) 292-7900
www.kuninfelt.com

Lion Brand Yarn Co.
34 W. 15th St.
New York, NY 10011
(800) 795-5466

Rainbow Gallery
Mail-order source:
Designs by Joan Green
3897 Indian Ridge Woods
Oxford, OH 45056
(513) 523-0437
(Mon–Fri., 9 a.m.–5 p.m.)

Spinrite Inc.
P.O. Box 435
Lockport, NY 14094-0435
(800) 265-2864
or
Box 40
Listowel, Ontario N4W 3H3
Canada
(519) 291-3780

Uniek
Mail-order source:
Annie's Attic Catalog
1 Annie Ln.
Big Sandy, TX 75755
(800) 582-6643

**Westrim Crafts/Western
Trimming Corp.**
9667 Canoga Ave.
P.O. Box 3879
Chatsworth, CA 91311
(818) 998-8550